The New Tradition Cookbook

The New Tradition Cookbook

by

Valerie Hart

e d i t e c h   p r e s s   ■   m i a m i

First Edition

© 1988 by Valerie Hart

Library of Congress Catalog Card Number: 88-080109

ISBN 0-945586-01-9

Printed in the United States of America

This book is dedicated to the two men in my life:

ROYAL AND ROBERT

My Father, Royal, whose insatiable quest for knowledge extends into the wonderful world of food

and

My Husband, Robert (Buddy), whose love and patience encouraged me to continue creating new recipes, which he willingly endured.

Contents

Preface

My Grandparents' home remains illuminated in my mind's eye of childhood memories. The only hors d'oeuvre served was Beluga caviar. Large gray nuggets of divine pleasure from the Caspian Sea were spooned from a silver container and passed by their houseman, who had begun his service when my Mother was eleven years-old and remained with the family until his passing fifty-six years later. He always wore white when he served, including the gloves covering his hands. Toast points were passed as an accompaniment, but never egg, onion, or sour cream. One was to eat the tiny eggs with the runcible spoon provided while nibbling on the toast in-between. Champagne was poured even to the children, and, although we really didn't find it palatable, we were impressed to be included in such grown-up sociality.

My Grandparents lived in a world where gracious living was the practiced art of elegant women devoted to the career of home and family. It was not until I had reached my middle years that I discovered I was an anachronism, interposed between old values and new freedoms, tradition and liberation, unbending etiquette and absence of rules. Yet, in the face of the metamorphosis of the last years there is also a comforting permanency. Gracious living doesn't lie with caviar and white gloves but in the attitudes we inherit and present unspoken to the next generation. It is the joy of creating something special to share with family and friends. My Grandmother gave the best of herself and her home when she entertained and everyone present felt special to be a part of the occasion. In the face of unyielding schedules and a multi-faceted life it is necessary to remember this heritage. I have designed this book and created the recipes with enjoyment in mind. Although the recipes are based upon traditional Continental and American cuisine and range from elegant to ethnic they have been altered to concur with our lighter diets and busy time schedules. Those which take time to prepare can be frozen for later use, and the others can be accomplished quickly and easily. They are written as I cook and have taught them in my cooking classes with uncomplicated step by step directions so the reader doesn't have to interpret or change them to be workable.

I would like this book to become a comfortable friend for everyday usage as well as for company dinners. Hopefully, it will stand the test of time for my children to refer to with the knowledge it was written out of love—love of good foods—love of those who influenced my life—love of those yet to be born who will equate their past, my lifetime, with stability to pass onto their children.

Valerie Hart
Miami Beach, Florida
February 1988

A Favorite Toast to Our Guests

"May You Always Steal, Swear, Cheat, and Lie"

"Steal" away from bad company
"Swear" by your friends
"Cheat" the Devil. And
"Lie" with the one you love best.

Appetizers

Boursin Cheese

2 tablespoons butter, softened
1 large clove garlic
½ teaspoon dill weed
¼ teaspoon thyme
2 tablespoons minced parsley
1 tablespoon minced chives
8 ounces cream cheese, softened

1. Put all the ingredients except the cream cheese in a food processor or mash together well. Beat or stir in cream cheese.
2. Put into a small oiled mold and refrigerate overnight.
3. Unmold and grind black pepper over the top and sides. Serve with crisp crackers.

NOTE: *This may be kept in the refrigerator for a week. It should be made a day or two in advance so the flavors will "marry."*

Swiss Fondue

½ pound imported dry Emanthal Swiss cheese
½ pound imported Gruyère cheese
1 cup dry white wine
2 tablespoons cornstarch, dissolved in ½ cup cold water
4 tablespoons Kirschwasser brandy
Pepper and nutmeg to taste

1. Crumble cheeses and put them into the top of a double boiler.
2. Add wine and stir. Bring water under double boiler to a boil and stir occasionally until cheeses are melted.
3. Mix cornstarch with a little cold water and stir into cheese mixture until smooth and creamy. Lower heat to medium.
4. Stir in Kirschwasser and cook, stirring, for 5 minutes. Put into fondue pot.
5. Serve with a good French bread cut into squares.

NOTE: *If mixture separates and the wine rises to the top, add a bit more cornstarch and stir.*

The proper fondue pot is made out of clay but is difficult to find in this country. Stainless steel ones may be found in most gourmet shops.

Mushroom Rolls Hors d'Oeuvre

1 pound fresh mushrooms
1 large onion
½ cup butter
1 loaf soft white bread, crusted and rolled thin with a rolling pin
1 cup butter
2 cookie sheets

1. Chop mushrooms and onion fine by hand. If you use the food processor be careful not to pulverize the ingredients.
2. Sauté in ¼ cup butter
3. Pour off all liquid through a colander.
4. Melt remaining butter in a saucepan.
5. Butter the cookie sheets, or set a layer of parchment paper on top. For each slice of bread you will use 1 tablespoon cooled mushroom mixture. Place mushroom mixture along the center of the bread and fold one side over. Brush a bit of the melted butter along the edge, and fold over the first half. Brush all over well with the melted butter and place flap side down onto the cookie sheet.
6. When finished with all the bread, trim the edges with a sharp knife and cut the rolls into halves.
7. Bake at 350° for 25 minutes, or until well-browned and crunchy.

NOTE: I have taught this to beginners for 20 years with a 100% success rate.

TO FREEZE: Make up a double or triple batch. Place rolls in a single layer on the cookie sheet. Do not cover until frozen. Transfer the frozen rolls with a spatula to a container to freeze indefinitely. Freeze each batch this way. When ready to cook, thaw completely and bake as above.

Stuffed Mushroom Caps

12 large mushrooms
1 large Bermuda onion
3 tablespoons butter
1 tablespoon flour
½ cup flaked and picked over crabmeat
2 tablespoons dry light sherry
1 tablespoon chopped parsley
Pepper to taste
Cornflake crumbs
Melted butter

1. Trim the stems from 12 large, uniform mushrooms and transfer the caps to a well-buttered or Teflon baking sheet.
2. Dice the onion fine with the stems and sauté over a medium-low fire in the butter until soft (about 5 minutes).
3. Mix the flour with the sherry in a cup and stir into the mixture.
4. Stir in the parsley. Sprinkle with pepper and stir until blended. Gently toss in the crabmeat with 2 forks without mashing it.
5. Fill the mushroom caps. Sprinkle each cap with cornflake crumbs and melted butter. Bake at 350° for 15 minutes.

NOTE: *These may be made in the morning, refrigerated, and baked at the last minute. This is also a lovely first course. Place 3 caps around a 7" salad plate over several leaves of fresh spinach or ridicchio.*

ABOUT MUSHROOMS: *The French tell you to wipe mushrooms with a cloth instead of washing them. Anything that is fertilized or sprayed or handled by someone else gets washed in my house. Do not ever soak mushrooms. Hold them individually under cold, running water and rub off any dirt. Cut off the very bottom of the stem and discard it. If the caps have turned slightly brown on top, peel off the outer layer, working from the outer edge carefully with your index finger and thumb or a very sharp paring knife. Buy only firm white mushrooms.*

Curried Herring

12-ounce bottle herring tidbits in wine, drained
1½ cups sour cream (12 ounces)
2 firm apples (Granny Smith or Jonathan)
3 tomatoes—peeled, seeded, and chopped
1 tablespoon curry powder
3 tablespoons chopped scallion greens
1 teaspoon finely-chopped dill weed
½ teaspoon hot Hungarian paprika or a pinch of cayenne pepper

1. Combine all the above and allow to marinate overnight. Serve very cold.

NOTE: *This is an excellent first course. Serve in a large lettuce leaf with a sliced hard boiled egg across the top and sprinkle lightly with regular paprika and a bit of chopped dill weed.*

Mussels with Gruyère Cheese and Vodka

Serves 6 people as a first course

48 mussels
2 ounces vodka
1 tablespoon oregano
4 whole garlic cloves
3 cups strong chicken broth
Bread crumbs seasoned with salt, pepper, and Parmesan cheese
½ pound finely-crumbled Gruyère cheese

1. Wash mussels well. Remove top shell leaving mussels in tact in bottom half.
2. Simmer whole garlic cloves and oregano in mixture of vodka and chicken broth for 15 minutes. Remove garlic cloves.
3. Put mussels in a shallow baking dish. Do not overlap. Cover with broth mixture. Bake, covered, for 10 minutes in a pre-heated 400° oven. Remove cover. Sprinkle lightly with bread crumbs and crumbled cheese. Broil until brown and bubbly.

Caponata

2 pounds eggplant, peeled and cut into ½" cubes
1½ teaspoons salt
½ cup olive oil (Italian)
1½ cups chopped onion, or if available, 3 shallots
¾ teaspoon minced garlic (1 large clove)
1 cup minced celery
6 finely-chopped anchovies
1½ cups thinly-sliced pimento-stuffed olives
1 cup coarsely-chopped black olives
½ cup capers
½ cup vodka
2 teaspoons sugar, dissolved in ½ cup red wine vinegar
4 fresh tomatoes, skinned, seeded, and chopped
1 6-ounce can tomato paste
½ teaspoon black pepper
½ teaspoon hot Hungarian paprika

1. Sprinkle eggplant cubes with salt and allow to stand at least 1 hour in ice water to cover. Drain and wash in cold water.
2. Heat oil and sauté onion, celery, and garlic until soft. Remove vegetables and place eggplant cubes in pan, stirring until lightly browned. Add more oil if necessary.
3. Return vegetables to pan with remaining ingredients and bring to a boil. Reduce heat and simmer 45 minutes. Refrigerate 3 days.

NOTE: *This is an unusual hors d'oeuvre which can be served with crackers, celery, or chips. It is also marvelous with tortillas or in pita bread.*

Creamy Escargot

Serves 6 people (6 apiece)

½ cup finely-chopped shallots (about 3)
¼ cup finely-chopped celery (1 stalk)
1 clove minced garlic
1 pound thinly-sliced small mushrooms
4 tablespoons butter
1 teaspoon tarragon
1 cup cream
1 beaten egg yolk
2 tablespoons minced parsley
36 large snails
2 tablespoons Pernod liqueur
Salt and pepper to taste
36 miniature escarcoques (patty shells), or 6 large shells.

1. Sauté shallots, celery, mushrooms, and garlic in the butter about 5 minutes, or until soft.
2. Add Pernod, tarragon, and parsley, and stir until blended.
3. Add the escargots.
4. Combine the cream with the beaten egg yolk and add slowly, stirring until very hot and thick. Add salt and pepper to your taste.
5. Spoon into patty shells on individual plates. Sprinkle with a little chopped parsley. Place a few cherry tomatoes in a leaf of ridicchio or endive on one side and serve immediately.

NOTE: The cooked patty shells should be put into a warmer or 250° oven to heat before filling.

Clams Oregano

24 medium-sized clams or mussels
½ cup butter
¼ cup finely-chopped celery
1 clove garlic, minced (not crushed)
2 tablespoons minced fresh parsley
1 teaspoon oregano
1 tablespoon vodka
¼ cup chicken broth
½ cup plain bread crumbs
⅛ teaspoon black pepper

1. Wash clams well. Open and remove from shells and chop. Reserve 12 shells.
2. Melt the butter and sauté the celery, garlic, parsley, oregano, and vodka over a low fire until celery is soft. Stir in the chicken broth, bread crumbs, and black pepper. Stir in the chopped clams and fill the shells. Place under a hot broiler (not too close) and cook until tops are very brown. Serve with a pimento strip across each clam.

NOTE: Clams are easier to open if you put them into a covered frying pan with a little bit of water to steam <u>just</u> until the muscle relaxes so you can slide a knife into the opening. Do not allow them to cook.

Seafood Antipasto

1 pound squid (calamari), well-cleaned and sliced into thin rings
    (white part only)
½ pound small shrimp, shelled and deveined
1 pound sea scallops, cut into halves or quarters
2 cups water
1 bay leaf
White bulbs from 6 scallions, sliced thin
Handful of parsley, chopped fine
1 teaspoon thyme
3 whole cloves garlic
¼ teaspoon salt
⅛ teaspoon black pepper

1. Bring water to a boil with the bay leaf, sliced bulbs, parsley, thyme, garlic, salt, and pepper. Boil hard for 5 minutes.
2. Add calamari rings and boil for 1 minute more. Add shrimp. When water just returns to a boil remove pot from stove. Stir in scallops. Drain off the water and remove the garlic cloves and bay leaf.

6 green spring scallions
1 green pepper
1 fresh red pepper
¼ cup sliced pimento green olives
¼ cup pitted and sliced black Greek olives
⅔ cup good Italian olive oil
Juice from 1 lime
Freshly-ground black pepper to taste

1. Chop vegetables coarsely. Slice olives and toss into seafood. Pour in oil and squeeze lime over all. Toss. Salt and pepper to taste. Refrigerate several hours or overnight.

NOTE: This makes a delicious antipasto or buffet luncheon item, or dinner on a summer night.

Rolled Shrimp Hors d'Oeuvre

1 loaf sliced soft white bread, crusted and rolled thin
1 pound medium shrimp
4 tablespoons butter
1 tablespoon curry powder
1" piece fresh ginger, peeled and cut into half
2 large cloves garlic, peeled and cut into halves
¼ teaspoon brown mustard
2 tablespoons soy sauce
4 tablespoons white dry vermouth
2 tablespoons flour
1¼ cups (1 10-ounce can) concentrated chicken broth
2 tablespoons finely-chopped spring onion greens

1. Peel, clean, and chop and shrimp into small pieces. (Do not dice.)
2. Melt the butter and add the rest of the ingredients. Simmer over a low fire for 10 minutes, stirring often. Remove the garlic and ginger pieces.
3. Stir in the shrimp and cook for only a minute longer.
4. To complete: Follow the directions on page 00 for putting together the mushroom hors d'oeuvre or follow the directions for Spinach in Phyllo Dough to put into Phyllo Triangles for a first course or luncheon menu. These freeze beautifully both ways.

Deviled Lobster Puffs

1. Make a Pâte-à-Chou recipe, keeping puffs bite-sized.
2. Make lobster filling:
3. Melt butter. Stir in flour, cognac, cream and seasonings. Stir in lobster meat. Split and fill cream puffs. Put puffs onto a baking sheet and bake for 5–7 minutes at 350°.

1 7-ounce can lobster meat, or ¾ cup chopped fresh lobster meat
2 tablespoons butter
1 tablespoon flour
1 tablespoon cognac
¼ teaspoon dill weed
¼ teaspoon Dijon mustard
Pinch black pepper
⅓ cup light cream
¼ teaspoon grated Parmesan cheese
Tiny pinch cayenne pepper

NOTE: *Pâte-à-Chou may be made well in advance and frozen indefinitely.*

Duck Pâté

Livers from 6 Long Island ducklings
¼ pound butter
2 cloves garlic
1 large coarsely chopped onion
1 teaspoon thyme (scant)
1 bay leaf
½ pound Italian mild sausage, precooked and sliced
3 tablespoons brandy or cognac
1 tablespoon heavy cream

1. Melt butter and sauté whole garlic cloves for a few minutes over a low fire. Remove from the fire and allow to stand 15 minutes. Remove garlic cloves.
2. Return pan to fire and add chopped onion, sausage, thyme, bay leaf, and cook over medium-low fire until onion is soft. Stir in duck livers and brandy and continue to cook, turning over livers until done. (Do not overcook.) Remove bay leaf.
3. Cool and put into a food processor. Turn on/off several times until pulverized but not liquid purée. Put back into the pan and stir in heavy cream. (Do not heat.)
4. Put into a crock and top with the bay leaf. Refrigerate overnight. Serve with thin Danish black bread triangles.

Lobster Timbales

Yields 8 portions

8 4-ounce plastic cups
4 pounds live Maine lobster
3 cloves fresh garlic
1 bay leaf
2 teaspoons thyme
1 teaspoon dried basil or a bunch of fresh basil leaves
3 quarts water
1 cup Hellmann's mayonnaise (or, another pure mayonnaise)
½ teaspoon hot Hungarian paprika
½ teaspoon white horseradish
1 red pepper, 1 yellow pepper, and 1 green pepper, chopped fine
    by hand
1 tablespoon fresh dill weed, or 1 teaspoon dried dill weed
½ cup chopped chives or scallion greens
2 tablespoons (packets) unflavored gelatin, dissolved in ¼ cup cool
    water
½ cup broth from the lobsters

1. Bring the water to a boil with the basil, thyme, bay leaf, and
   garlic cloves. Plunge the lobsters into the water as follows:

1 pound "chicks"	=	12 minutes
1½ pounders	=	15 minutes
2 pounders or over	=	20 minutes

   (The timing begins after the water returns to a boil with the
   lobsters in it)
2. Remove lobsters from water immediately and allow to cool for
   10 minutes. Continue boiling the water for ½ hour. Remove all
   meat and cut into small pieces.
3. Combine mayonnaise, paprika, horseradish, chopped red,
   yellow, and green peppers, dill, and chives.
4. Dissolve gelatin in ¼ cup cool water and stir in ½ cup of the
   lobster broth. Allow to cool for 10 minutes before stirring into
   the mayonnaise mixture.
5. Add the lobster pieces and spoon into the cups. Refrigerate all
   day or overnight.

6. Work a knife around the inside of the cup to loosen the molds and turn out onto lettuce, ridicchio, or endive. Put a slice of green pimento olive onto the top of each and decorate the plate with olives, cherry tomatoes, and dill sprigs.

NOTE: This is an elegant first course, particularly during the summer months.

5-ounce plastic cup   (Exact size)

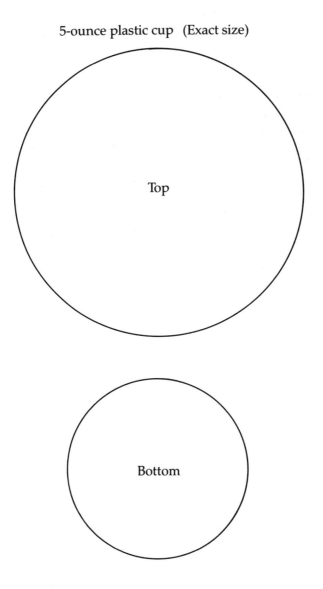

Top

Bottom

Steak Cubes Teriyaki for Fondue

2 pounds sirloin, cut into ¼" squares
¼ cup peanut or Grapeseed oil
½ cup soya sauce
½ cup dry light sherry
1 tablespoon ground ginger
2 tablespoons white sugar
1½ teaspoons powdered or 2 cloves fresh garlic, split into halves
1 large minced onion
1 tablespoon minced fresh parsley

1. Marinate the meat in the above for several hours or overnight turning several times.
2. Serve on skewers placed around a fondue pot filled with hot peanut or grapeseed oil for the guests to make their own hors d'oeuvre.
3. Put extra marinade in a small warmer on the side.

NOTE: Make sure meat is bite-sized for easy handling. This same recipe can be used for a casual dinner. Serve a good French or Italian bread on the side with a large tossed salad.

Steak Tartare

Super Good

1 pound filet of beef, very lean, ground or scraped immediately
  before use
2 tablespoons capers
1 small onion
2 drops Tabasco sauce
6 drops Worcestershire sauce
1 clove garlic
3 anchovy fillets
½ teaspoon black pepper
1 tablespoon ketchup
1 tablespoon minced parsley
1 tablespoon cognac (optional)
Toast points
Mustard
Combination of fresh chives, capers, anchovy, and parsley for
  garnish

1. Combine all of the ingredients except the meat in a food processor or blender and purée.
2. Blend with the ground filet and form into an attractive mound on a glass platter.
3. Garnish and surround with parsley and egg yolks, which have been put back into their shells and sprinkled with paprika.
4. Serve with toastpoints which have been spread lightly with mustard.

NOTE: Steak tartare must be from the best cut of beef and must always be fresh. If any is left over, form into meatballs and cook.

Watercress Hors d'Oeuvre

1 loaf soft white bread
4 seeded and finely-chopped cucumbers
1 bunch chopped watercress leaves
3 ounces cream cheese, room temperature
1 teaspoon salt
½ teaspoon white pepper
1 bunch watercress, washed and drained
¼ pound unsalted butter at room temperature

1. Chop cucumbers and watercress. Add salt and pepper and place in a strainer for one hour to drain water.
2. Mash cream cheese into watercress mixture.
3. Crust bread slices.
4. Spread butter onto one side of bread.
5. Spoon watercress mixture onto bread and turn one side of the bread over mixture and then the other side of the bread over the first, pressing slightly so the butter will adhere to the bread. Turn flap side down on platter (so they will not open). Push a sprig of fresh watercress into the end of each.
6. Decorate platter with whole watercress. Refrigerate covered with a plastic wrap. They should be served very cold as an appetizer, tea sandwich, or accompaniment to a luncheon plate.

Soup

Split Pea Soup

6 quarts water
1 large hambone (reserved from leftover cooked ham) or 6 smoked
    ham hocks
Diced ham
6 whole cloves
3 large leeks, white part only, chopped, or 1 huge finely-chopped
    onion
2 cloves finely-chopped garlic
1 teaspoon black pepper
2 teaspoons salt
2 whole bay leaves
1 teaspoon thyme
Quick-cooking dried green split peas (12-ounce package)

1. Reserve diced ham to add later.
2. Bring the rest of the ingredients to a boil and reduce heat to medium. Cook 2 hours, covered. Remove hambone or hocks and continue cooking for another hour and a half. Add diced ham. Allow to cool for several hours in order for the flavors to settle and the soup to thicken. Reheat and serve.

NOTE: The longer the soup cooks or stands, the thicker it becomes. If it is refrigerated overnight, it may become too thick when reheated. If so, add water, stirring until blended.

*   May be served with a small glass of dry sherry on the side to drink or to pour into the hot soup.*

Cream of Spinach Soup

Serves 4 people

1 pound fresh spinach leaves
1 minced onion
Handful of parsley
1 cup milk
¼ teaspoon dried tarragon
¼ teaspoon nutmeg
1 crushed garlic clove
½ teaspoon salt
½ teaspoon pepper
1 cup heavy cream
Pinch of cayenne pepper
Fresh spinach leaves for garnish

1. Combine first 9 ingredients and simmer for ½ hour. Cool a bit and purée in the food processor or blender. Return to the pot and stir in the heavy cream. Taste for salt and pepper and, if you like a zing, put in a pinch of cayenne pepper. Bring almost to the boiling point, pour into individual cups or a tureen and stir in large pieces of raw spinach leaves.

Cold Cucumber Soup

Serves 4 people

2 10-ounce cans Campbell's Chicken Broth
2 cans water
2 potatoes, skinned and sliced
1 large clove garlic
1 large onion or 2 leeks
½ teaspoon black pepper
1 bay leaf
½ teaspoon thyme
½ teaspoon dill
1 whole clove
1 large or 2 medium cucumbers
Fresh chives or scallion greens
Salt, if you wish

1. Bring all to a boil in a soup pot. Cover and reduce heat to medium. Boil gently for 1 hour. Cool.
2. Pour a little at a time into a blender and purée. Pour into a glass container.
3. Skin, seed, and chop cucumbers coarse. Chop scallions or chives. Stir into the soup and refrigerate until very cold. Sprinkle more chives on top to serve. If you like it creamy, stir in ¼ cup plain yogurt or sour cream just before serving.

Vichyssoise

1 medium onion, sliced
4 leeks, white bulb only, sliced thin
1 stalk celery, sliced
¼ cup sweet butter
5 medium potatoes, thinly-sliced
1 quart chicken broth
1 tablespoon salt
1 teaspoon white pepper
3 cups milk
2 cups heavy cream
Chopped chives
Black caviar

1. Cook the vegetables in the butter until golden in color.
2. Add the potatoes, broth, and seasoning, and boil 35 minutes.
3. Purée in blender or food processor.
4. Return mixture to the pot. Add the milk and 1 cup of the cream. Bring almost to a boil, stirring constantly with a wooden spoon so soup will not burn at the bottom.
5. Correct the seasoning.
6. Strain into a bowl or plastic container, pushing as much of the thickness through as possible. Add the remaining cream and chill overnight.
7. May be made 2 days ahead. Garnish with chives and a dollop of caviar.

Won Ton Soup

Serves 6 people

Won Ton

1½ cups sifted all-purpose flour
1 teaspoon salt
1 egg, slightly beaten
⅓ cup water

1. Mix flour and salt. Add egg and water. Stir with a wire whisk.
2. Turn out on a floured board. Knead to make a soft smooth dough. Cover with a clean towel and let rest 15 minutes.
3. Roll dough out paper thin into a rectangle (about 8″ × 12″). Sprinkle with more flour as needed to prevent dough from sticking. Cut into 24 two-inch squares. Leave on board while preparing meat mixture.

Filling for Won Ton

¼ pound cooked pork, chicken, or shrimp, chopped fine
½ teaspoon salt
Pinch of pepper
2 teaspoons minced green onions
2 quarts boiling, salted water

1. Mix chopped meat, salt, pepper, and onions together.
2. Place a spoonful of mixture in the center of each square of dough. Fold diagonally in half. Press edges firmly together to seal.
3. Drop into boiling water. Cook 15 minutes. Drain. Keep warm.

Soup for Won Ton

4 cups strong chicken broth
½ cup minced celery
½ cup sliced bamboo shoots
6 fresh white mushrooms
½ cup shredded cooked chicken
1 cup tightly-packed washed raw spinach leaves

1. Prepare soup by putting broth into a saucepan. Add celery. Bring to a boil. Reduce heat and cook 5 minutes.
2. Add chicken, bamboo shoots, mushrooms, and spinach leaves. Remove from fire immediately.
3. Put 4 won tons in each soup bowl. Pour soup over.

Minnesota Wild Rice and Mushroom Soup

6-ounce box of wild rice
3 onions
½ cup dried mushrooms (Porcini from Italy, if available)
2 quarts beef broth (or, 5 10-ounce cans Campbell's Beef Bouillon, undiluted)
1 pound fresh mushrooms
Salt and pepper to taste

1. Pour boiling water over the rice and allow to stand overnight to cool. In the morning pour off the water and wash the rice in cold water in a colander.
2. Chop the onions fine.
3. Soak the dried mushrooms in hot water for 15 minutes. Pour off the water and wash. Chop into coarse pieces.
4. Combine the rice, onions, dried mushrooms, and beef broth in a soup pot and bring to a boil. Reduce heat to low. Cover, and boil gently for 1½ hours.
5. Clean and slice the fresh mushrooms as thin as possible and add them to the soup. Continue boiling ½ hour longer. Add salt and pepper to taste. Serve with a good fresh black bread.

Shrimp and Crab Bisque

Serves 8 people

4 cups water
2 pounds raw blue crab, cleaned and cut into quarters
Shells from 1 pound raw small shrimp (reserve shrimp for later)
The bottom from 1 whole bunch celery
2 large onions, cut into quarters
2 cloves garlic, split
2 bay leaves
1 teaspoon thyme
1 teaspoon oregano

1. Bring the above to a boil. Cover. Reduce heat to medium and boil gently for ½ hour. Cool completely.
2. Strain into another pot. Pick over the crab shells to gather all the meat possible and add it to the strained stock.

2 10-ounce cans Campbell's Zesty Tomato Soup
1 10-ounce can Campbell's Gazpacho Soup
½ cup finely-chopped scallion greens
1 teaspoon hot Hungarian paprika
¼ cup heavy sherry or Port wine
Reserved shrimp from shells
½ cup heavy cream

1. Stir the Campbell's soups into the strained stock until very smooth. Add the paprika and the sherry and cook over a low fire for 10 minutes. This may be done in the morning.
2. Just before serving, bring soup to a boil, stirring so it will not burn on the bottom. Stir in the raw shrimp. Turn fire off immediately. Stir in the cream and serve immediately.

NOTE: You may top each bowl with croutons.

Curry Gumbo

A Big Pot: Serves 6 people

2 quarts water
1 large coarsely-chopped onion
1 coarsely-chopped green pepper
1 piece coarsely-chopped celery
2 tablespoons chopped fresh parsley
2 bay leaves
1 teaspoon curry powder (or more at the end for a stronger flavor)
1 teaspoon salt
1 teaspoon thyme
1 teaspoon chili powder
2 15-ounce cans stewed tomatoes
2 potatoes, cut the size of the shrimp

---

1 pound lobster meat, raw, chopped coarse
½ cup chopped cooked ham or spicy sausage
12 raw clams in their shells
2½ cups sliced fresh okra, or 1 15-ounce can
1 pound medium-sized shrimp, shelled and cleaned, left whole
12 oysters, shucked in advance, with their liquid

1. Put the first 12 ingredients (up to the line) in a large pot and boil uncovered for 45 minutes over a medium-high fire.
2. Add the lobster meat and cook 15 minutes more over a medium fire.
3. Add the ham-sausage and clams and cook until the clams open (about 5 minutes).
4. Stir in the okra and shrimp for 1 minute.
5. Stir in the oysters and serve immediately.

NOTE: Cooked rice may also be added to the gumbo. Any firm fish may be substituted for the lobster or added to the gumbo for reasons of economy or flavor.

Manhattan Clam Chowder

4 dozen large clams
1 large finely-chopped onion
1 piece finely-chopped celery
1 finely-chopped green pepper
Fat from 3 slices cooked bacon (crumble bacon and reserve)
2 large potatoes, cut into cubes
1 bay leaf
1 teaspoon Italian herb seasoning (McCormick or Spice Islands)
1 29-ounce can of chopped tomatoes and their juice
2 cups water
Juice from the clams

1. Scrub the clams very well to remove all sand. Steam them in a large pot in 6 cups water until the shells pop open. Do not overcook. Remove the clams from the water, reserving the juice.
2. Cut the clams into small pieces, removing or finely chopping the hard round muscle at the end.
3. Sauté the onion, celery and pepper in a soup pot in the bacon fat and cook until soft. Add all the other ingredients except the clams and bring to a boil. Cover and lower the fire to medium. Boil gently for 30 minutes. Add the clams. Correct the seasoning. Serve with chowder biscuits or pilot crackers.

Fish

Smoked Fish Mousse

1 cup light cream
1½ pounds smoked fish
1 tablespoon minced dill weed
½ cup minced parsley
3 tablespoons unflavored gelatin
⅓ cup cool water
3 tablespoons butter or margarine
3 tablespoons flour
1 small minced onion
2 cups milk
1 teaspoon nutmeg
¼ cup heavy cream, whipped with 1 teaspoon sugar
½ teaspoon black pepper

1. Put fish, cream, dill, and parsley into the food processor and pulverize.
2. Combine gelatin and water and set aside.
3. Melt the butter (margarine). Add the onion and sauté over a low fire until soft. Stir in the flour and, very slowly, the milk until smooth and thick. Add the nutmeg and pepper. Stir in the gelatin. Remove from the fire. Cool. Fold in the whipped cream.
4. Fold in the fish mixture and spoon into an oiled one quart mold. Refrigerate until cold. Unmold. Serve surrounded by crackers.

NOTE: *This is unique and very, very good. The better the fish and the harder it is smoked, the better the mousse.*

Fillet of Sole Suchet

Serves 4 people

Fish Stuffing

½ pound ground sole
1 egg white, beaten until frothy
¼ cup heavy cream
¼ teaspoon salt
⅛ teaspoon pepper

1. Combine the above and set aside.

Fillet Preparation

4 fillets of sole, boned and skinned
Salt and pepper
½ cup white wine
Juice from ½ lemon
2 carrots
1 tablespoon butter
½ cup sherry or Madeira wine
2 fresh tomatoes

1. Peel and cut the carrots into fine strips and put into a pan with the butter and sherry. Cover and simmer until tender.
2. Spread the fillets with the stuffing. Fold into halves and place into a shallow baking dish. Add the wine and lemon juice and cover with buttered wax paper. Bake in a 350° oven for 10–15 minutes, or until a fork inserted separates the flesh easily.
3. Strain the liquid from the baked fish and reserve.

Béchamel Sauce

2 tablespoons butter
1 minced shallot
2 tablespoons flour
1 cup milk
2 tablespoons cream
Salt and pepper to taste

1. Melt the butter and cook the shallot for a few minutes. Stir in the flour and slowly add the milk and cream, stirring until very thick. Season with salt and pepper.
2. Stir in the reserved liquid from the fish and simmer to a creamy consistency, stirring constantly.

To Serve:

Arrange the fillets onto a heated serving dish, pour the sauce over, and garnish with the carrots and broiled tomato halves.

Shrimp Stuffing Variation

1 finely-chopped shallot
¼ teaspoon white pepper
¼ teaspoon dill weed
¼ teaspoon salt
Juice of ½ lemon
1 teaspoon minced parsley
½ pound small cleaned and chopped shrimp
1 beaten egg
¼ cup fine breadcrumbs

1. Sauté shallots in two tablespoons butter. Add the seasonings and shrimp and toss briefly until shrimp are barely cooked. Remove from fire. Toss in the beaten egg and breadcrumbs.
2. Fill the fillets as for Suchet or roll them around the shrimp mixture, securing with a toothpick. Follow the Suchet directions for baking and serving.

Fillet of Sole Véronique

1½ cups seedless or canned green grapes
1 cup dry white sherry

1. Peel the grapes and soak them in the sherry.
2. Add to the Béchamel Sauce and pour over the fillets.

A Fish in Thyme

1 small firm-fleshed fish of your choice, cleaned, skinned, and
    filleted into 2 pieces
Salt and pepper
¾ cup canned concentrated chicken broth
Juice from ¼ lemon
¼ pound mushrooms, sliced (canned or fresh)
A bit of fresh parsley, chopped
½ teaspoon dried chervil
1 teaspoon dried thyme

1. Combine the chicken broth, lemon juice, onion, mushrooms, parsley, thyme, and chervil in a pan and bring to a boil.
2. Lightly salt and pepper the fish fillets and add them to the pan. Reduce the heat to medium. Cover the pan and cook for about 10 minutes, or until the flesh is white and separates easily with a fork. Do not overcook.
3. Serve with red pepper, carrot and zucchini strips, which have been steamed with a bay leaf.

Tuscan Tuna

2 13-ounce cans white meat tuna
1 3½-ounce jar capers
1 2-ounce can anchovies
1 teaspoon dill weed
6 pieces celery
Handful of parsley
½ lemon
6 hard cooked eggs
Salt and pepper to taste
Mayonnaise
Sliced pimento olives

1. Put the tuna into the food processor with the steel blade and pulverize. Empty into a large bowl.
2. Put the capers and anchovies into the processor with the parsley and the juice from the lemon. Purée. Empty into the bowl containing the tuna.
3. Put the celery and dill into the processor and pulverize. Add to tuna.
4. Put the eggs into the processor and pulverize. Add to tuna.
5. Add salt and pepper to taste, and enough mayonnaise to bind.
6. Fold in sliced olives.
7. Spread onto a platter (not silver) and decorate with homemade mayonnaise piped through a fluted tip of a piping tube.
8. Decorate with capers, pimento strips, green asparagus, sliced pimento olives, anchovies, deviled eggs, artichoke hearts, or anything else that suits you.

NOTE: This recipe becomes the "Tonnato" topping for Vitello Tonnato.

Italian Baked Fish

1 firm fish, such as Snapper or Bass, head and tail intact
Fresh rosemary sprigs
Fresh basil leaves
Garlic cloves, peeled and left whole
Lemon juice
Olive oil
Light dry sherry
Salt, pepper, Hungarian paprika

1. Preheat over to 400°.
2. Clean the fish inside and remove the scales. With a small paring knife, make a slit along both sides of the bone at the tail section.
3. Spread a large piece of heavy duty aluminum foil on a large flat cookie sheet. Brush it with oil.
4. Salt fish well inside and place rosemary, basil and garlic all along the inside, inserting them into the cut tail section. Squeeze the juice of one lemon over the inside and brush with about ½ cup sherry, or until moistened.
5. Close fish and salt and heavily pepper skin on both sides. Brush heavily with olive oil. Sprinkle with paprika. Bring up edges of foil, tent style, keeping fish flat and seal by tightly folding edges into each other without touching the top of the fish. Seal ends so no air escapes.
6. Place in a preheated 375° oven and bake as follows:

1½ pound fish	=	15 minutes	=	2 people
3-pound fish	=	25 minutes	=	4 people
5½ pound fish	=	40 minutes	=	6 people
7½ pound fish	=	40 minutes	=	8 people

7. When the fish is done, carefully open the foil. Loosen the bottom of the fish with a spatula and slide the whole fish onto a large platter with the help of two spatulas. Remove the eyes and place a black olive into each socket. Encircle the olives with a narrow strip of pimento. Decorate the platter with bunches of watercress, cherry tomatoes (left whole and peeled), and huge shrimp which have been steamed with garlic and bay leaf,

shelled, and cleaned. Bring the platter to the table for display, and then portion the fish from a side table onto individual plates.
8. Accompany the fish with whole unpeeled red potatoes and a medley of julienned fresh vegetables.

Fruited Fish Key West Style

Serves 2 people

2 fresh, white-fleshed fish fillets, boned and skinned
Juice from ½ lime
1 tablespoon honey
1 cup chicken broth
¼ teaspoon powdered ginger
1 teaspoon curry powder
1 tablespoon light soy sauce
Chinese pea pods
Mango slices or sliced skinned peaches
Whole tiny red potatoes

1. Cut a strip around each potato and boil in a little water until done but not too soft. (The reason you cut a strip around is not only to create a pretty design, but also to keep the skin from popping.)
2. Combine the lime juice, honey, chicken broth, thyme, curry, and soy sauce in a pan and bring to a boil, stirring. Remove from the fire. Cool.
3. Place the fish fillets in the sauce. Cover the pan and poach over medium heat for about 10 minutes, or until the fish flakes when touched with a fork. Do not overcook.
4. Add the pea pods to the pan and spoon the hot sauce over without cooking them.
5. Remove fillets to 2 plates and arrange the pea pods, the potatoes, and the sliced mango or peaches around.

NOTE: When we first ate this in Key West, I couldn't figure out the ingredients. The combination of the mango and the curry with the ginger and honey is an incredible taste sensation.

Chinese-Style Poached Fish

1 4–5 pound firm, white-fleshed fish
2 tablespoons soy sauce
½ cup oil
2 tablespoons finely-sliced gingerroot
2 cloves finely-sliced garlic
3 scallions, cut into 1½" pieces
2 tablespoons sherry or rice wine
1 teaspoon arrowroot

1. Put enough water in a skillet or fish poacher to cover the fish. Bring to a boil. Gently place the whole, cleaned fish into the water. Cover and boil gently for about 10 minutes, or until fish feels firm when touched.
2. Carefully remove fish to heatproof platter. Remove top skin. Leave head and tail in tact. Sprinkle with soy sauce.
3. In a small saucepan, heat oil and add the remaining ingredients, except arrowroot. Cook about 2 minutes on medium fire.
4. Remove from heat. Stir in arrowroot. Mixture will thicken slightly into a clear gravy.
5. Pour over warm fish. Serve hot or warm on a large platter well decorated.

Traditional Gefülte Fish

Makes 8 good-sized balls

Fish Stock

1 large soup pot
3–4 stalks celery with leaves
2 onions, cut into quarters
A big handful of fresh parsley
A handful of fresh dill
1 large clove garlic
1 bay leaf
2 teaspoons salt
2 teaspoons white pepper
Head, bones, and skin of fish
16 cups water (1 gallon)

1. Boil the ingredients for the fish stock together in the soup pot for 1½ hours. Cool in the pot for 1 hour. Strain. Return strained stock to pot and discard the rest. Make fish balls.

Fish Balls

3 pounds firm whitefish; head, bones, and skin removed
1 pound trout or pike
2 large shallots
1 teaspoon white pepper
⅓ cup cold seltzer water or club soda
¼ cup matzo meal, unsifted, or ¼ cup fine breadcrumbs
3 egg whites

1. Grind together (or, put into food processor with steel blade) raw fish flesh, shallots, salt, pepper, matzo meal, and seltzer.
2. Beat egg whites stiff and fold into mixture.
3. Bring the fish stock to a boil. Roll fish into oblongs 4″ × 2″ and drop them into the stock. Turn the stock to medium and boil gently 1 hour, (partially covered so balls don't turn brown on top).
4. Let cool in fish stock, covered. Remove balls with a slotted spoon.
5. Dissolve 1 tablespoon unflavored gelatin in lukewarm water and stir into the fish stock. Bring to a boil and stir well. Allow to cool to room temperature and pour stock over fish balls. Cover tightly. Refrigerate overnight.
6. Cook 8 carrots. Split them in half lengthwise or slice into large pieces with serrated carrot slicer. Serve fish on individual plates over lettuce with the carrots, or arrange attractively on a platter. Garnish with fresh dill sprigs and accompany with beet horseradish.

German Fish Dumplings

Fischklösschen

2 pounds scrod, boned, skinned, and filleted (or any other
   white fish)
1 teaspoon salt
½ teaspoon pepper
1 teaspoon dill
1 teaspoon thyme
4 medium or 3 large shallots (or 1 large Bermuda onion)
2 cloves crushed garlic
2 egg yolks
½ cup ice water
½ cup fine breadcrumbs
2 egg whites, beaten stiff
4 10-ounce cans Campbell's Chicken Broth or, 6 cups strong
   homemade
6 cups water

1. Combine salt, pepper, dill, thyme, shallots, and crushed garlic
   in food processor and pulverize with steel blade.
2. Add fish, cut into chunks, and pulverize.
3. Add egg yolks and turn on/off until blended.
4. Add breadcrumbs and turn on/off until blended.
5. Beat egg whites stiff and fold in by hand or turn on/off quickly
   in processor.
6. Bring water and broth to a boil. Form fish into oblong balls
   about 4″ long by 2″ wide and drop into the broth. When it
   returns to a boil, turn fire to medium-low and partially cover
   with the pot top. Gently boil for 25 minutes. Cool in the broth
   overnight so the flavors will marry.
7. In a separate saucepan or skillet melt ¼ pound butter and sauté
   1 pound fresh mushrooms thickly sliced until soft. Stir in 2
   tablespoons flour and 5 cups of the broth from the fish and stir
   until smooth and slightly thickened.
8. Heat the fish dumplings in the remainder of the broth. Remove
   with a slotted spoon and pour the mushroom gravy over all.

Curried Salmon Nouvelle

Serves 4 people as a first course

2 cups canned or fresh, cooked salmon, left in chunks
Juice from ½ lemon
3 tablespoons butter or margarine
1 small diced onion
2 tablespoons diced celery
4 tablespoons flour
1 tablespoon curry powder, or more to taste
1 cup chicken broth
1 cup hot milk or cream
⅛ teaspoon pepper
1 large firm, ripe avocado
Pimento strips to decorate

1. Squeeze lemon juice over the salmon and make sure all bones have been removed.
2. Melt butter and sauté the onion and celery until soft. Remove pan from heat and stir in the flour. Stir in curry powder and chicken broth slowly with a wooden spoon and wire whisk until thick and smooth. Return to fire.
3. Add milk or cream slowly, continuing to stir until thick and smooth. Stir in pepper.
4. Stir in salmon chunks carefully.
5. Create rice molds by tightly packing a miniature soufflé cup or a 5-ounce paper cup with cooked rice. Turn upside down onto the center of individual plates or place in the center of a large round platter, and spoon curried salmon around.
6. Slice the avocado into thin strips and decorate the top of the salmon. Place pimento strips on top of the avocado strips in criss-cross fashion.

NOTE: *Cubed, cooked chicken may be substituted for the salmon.*

Salmon Mousse

2 cups (16 ounces) flaked, cooked or canned salmon
½ cup heavy cream
½ cup sour cream
2 tablespoons finely chopped chives or tops of green spring onions
1 tablespoon (package) unflavored gelatin
Juice of ½ lemon
½ cup chicken broth
2 chopped dill pickles
½ teaspoon white horseradish
¼ cup finely-diced celery
2 tablespoons pimento, cut into strips
Pinch cayenne pepper
½ teaspoon salt
1 teaspoon Pernod

1. Whip the cream thick. Add the sour cream and chives.
2. Dissolve the gelatin in the lemon juice. Add the lemon. Place over hot water to dissolve completely. Stir into cream mixture.
3. Add horseradish and salmon and beat until smooth.
4. Add the rest of the ingredients and put into an oiled mold.
5. Refrigerate until firm. Garnish with cucumbers, stuffed pimento olives on lettuce leaves.

Whole Poached Salmon

1 whole salmon, 6–7 pounds, cleaned with skin, bones, head and tail in tact

Court Bouillon

1 teaspoon green peppercorns (bottled in vinegar)
1 bay leaf
1 sliced onion
2 whole cloves
½ teaspoon celery seed
1 teaspoon salt
Juice of ½ lemon
Handful of parsley
8 cups water (or, to cover)
Roasting pan or fish poacher

1. Put the ingredients for court bouillon in the roaster or fish poacher and boil on top of the stove for 10 minutes. Allow to cool.
2. Wrap salmon in a double layer of cheesecloth with extra cloth on top. Place in court bouillon and cover.
3. Place in a preheated 350° oven and cook for 35–40 minutes. (When the area around the "cheek" flakes when touched by a knife, it is done.)
4. Carefully remove fish to a platter by picking up from the top by the extra cheesecloth. Open the cheesecloth carefully and roll onto a long platter. Carefully peel off the skin from the top. Leave the skin on the bottom and remove the eyes with a small spoon. Cool completely. Cover and refrigerate overnight or until very cold.
5. Make Cucumber/Dill Sauce.
6. Decorate salmon by putting a black olive in each eye socket. Create a ring around the eye with pimento strips. Surround the salmon with thin slices of unpeeled cucumber, sliced hard boiled eggs, capers, lemon, and, if you're adventuresome, pipe homemade mayonnaise in strips over the fish. Serve the Cucumber/Dill Sauce on the side in a gravy boat.

Cucumber/Dill Sauce

1 cup finely-chopped fresh chives or greens from scallions
½ cup watercress
1 cup parsley
3 teaspoons fresh dill weed
Juice of ½ lemon
1 cup seeded and diced cucumber
2 tablespoons tiny capers
1 teaspoon white horseradish
2 cups sour cream
½ teaspoon black pepper
½ teaspoon salt

1. Put the first 5 ingredients in the blender and purée. Fold in the cucumber, the sour cream, the capers, the horseradish, the salt and pepper. Spoon into a bowl or gravy boat. Decorate with watercress and serve as an accompaniment to seafood.

Alligator Tail

1 alligator tail, cut from an alligator measuring not more than 3'
2 tablespoons olive oil
Juice from 1 lemon
¼ pound butter
1 finely-chopped red pepper
2 minced shallots
½ teaspoon thyme
¼ teaspoon pepper
2 tablespoons dry white vermouth

1. Slice alligator tail very thin on the diagonal.
2. Squeeze the lemon juice over and toss well. Brush with the olive oil.
3. Cover and put into the refrigerator for at least 1 hour.
4. Sauté the pepper and shallots in the butter until soft. Add the thyme and pepper. Salt to taste. Add the vermouth. Stir in the slices of alligator and cover the pan. Simmer over a very low fire for 20 minutes.
5. Spoon over crusted toast points and serve immediately.

NOTE: Decorate the plates with small tomatoes, stuffed with bread crumbs or sautéed mushrooms or just decorated with sprigs of watercress for color.

This recipe is not inserted as a joke. If available, alligator is truly a delicacy. I also make it by following the first three steps and then combining:

¾ cup fine bread crumbs
¾ cup flour
1 cup light cream or half and half
3 beaten eggs

1. Dip the sliced tail into the batter and line them separately onto a sheet of waxed paper in the refrigerator for at least one hour. Melt half-butter half-olive oil to cover the bottom of a skillet. Sauté the cold pieces until lightly browned and serve with tartar sauce.

NOTE: Don't tell your guests what you have served them until they have tasted it and asked. I guarantee you a fun evening!

Shellfish

Clams

There are over 20,000 different kinds of clams throughout the world. However, only about 50 varieties are sufficiently large, tasty, and abundant enough to be fished commercially. The most abundantly obtained clam in the United States is the Eastern Surf Clam, which may be found along the coast from Maine to South Carolina. There are two varieties of clam: the hard-shelled clam and the soft-shelled clam. The hard-shelled clam, or quahog, is popular served either raw on the half shell, or minced in hot chowders. Small quahogs, usually served raw on the half shell, are called "cherry-stones." Their even smaller cousins are popularly called "littlenecks." The soft-shelled, or steamer, clam has a somewhat thin shell and a long, tubular sheath around its siphon.

Along the Pacific Coast are a number of sand-dwelling, shallow-water clams which grow as large as five pounds. The Indo-Pacific area claims a clam that weighs as much as 500 pounds with a length of 50 inches. The edible clams along the Pacific Coast are called "butter clams," which are absolutely fabulous. The several hundred species of freshwater clams which live in the Mississippi river are most beautiful with their greenish-black shells, but they are not edible.

The most important point to stress when working with clams and oysters is that they must be alive and healthy, and must come from unpolluted waters. Here are some pointers:

1. Buy only from a reputable source.
2. Scrub each one under cold running water to wash away the sand.
3. While you are washing them, check to see if each one is alive. The clam should be tightly shut. If it is not, tap it with your fingernail. If it does not snap shut, discard it. It is a sign that it does not react to external stimuli, which means it is dead.
4. Discard any clam which refuses to open after you have steamed or cooked it for ten minutes. Don't take any chances!
5. When the clams are very large, I remove the tough round muscle at the top after cooking, for it is difficult to chew and swallow.

Coquille St. Jacques

Serves 4 people

8 tablespoons (½ cup) butter or margarine
8 mushrooms cut into quarters
1 tablespoon minced parsley
1 tablespoon minced shallot
Pinch nutmeg
½ pound raw shrimp, cut into halves
½ pound scallops (if large, cut into halves or thirds)
3 tablespoons butter
3 tablespoons flour
½ teaspoon salt
¼ teaspoon white pepper
2 tablespoons light dry sherry
¾ cup milk
¾ cup heavy cream
⅛ cup mixed grated Romano and Parmesan cheese

1. Melt the butter and sauté the mushrooms, parsley, shallot and nutmeg until the mushrooms are soft.
2. Add the shrimp and toss in mushroom mixture until semi-cooked and coated.
3. Melt the 3 tablespoons butter. Stir in flour. Slowly stir in milk and cream. Add the grated cheese, and finally, the sherry. Taste. Correct the seasoning with salt and white pepper.
4. Add the shrimp/mushroom mixture to the white sauce. Remove from the heat.
5. Cut up the scallops and squeeze ½ lemon over them before serving.
6. Fill 4 ramekins with the shrimp/scallop mixture. Pipe potatoes around.
7. Mix together ½ cup fine bread crumbs with ¼ cup grated cheese. Sprinkle over the top of the coquille, but not over the potatoes.
8. Bake at 400° for 10 minutes, or until the potatoes show brown peaks and the coquille is bubbling.

Potatoes

4 large potatoes, skinned and boiled very soft
½ cup milk
2 teaspoons salt
½ teaspoon white pepper
Pinch nutmeg
1 tablespoon minced parsley

1. Put through a sieve into a piping bag with a fluted tube.

NOTE: *For 20 ramekins; buy 3 pounds medium-sized shrimp, 3 pounds scallops, and 40 mushrooms. Multiply the rest of the recipe by 4.*

Zuppa di Vongole

Serves 6 People

6 dozen cherrystone clams
12 skinned and chopped Italian plum tomatoes (To skin: Plunge
    tomatoes into a pot of boiling water for 30 seconds. Rinse under
    cold water while gently pulling off the outer skin.)
2 leaves chopped fresh basil or 1 tablespoon dried basil
2–3 cloves chopped fresh garlic
2 tablespoons chopped fresh parsley
1 teaspoon oregano
1 diced green pepper
1 diced sweet onion
2 pieces diced celery
2 cups canned thick tomato purée
Salt and pepper to taste
2 tablespoons Scotch whiskey

1. Sauté the vegetables and spices until soft in 2 tablespoons
   Italian olive oil. Stir in the tomato purée, salt, pepper, and
   Scotch.
2. Add the clams. Cover the pan and cook over a medium-low
   fire until they open.
3. Serve in individual soup dishes.

NOTE: *Two pounds shrimp may be substituted for the clams. Add the shrimp just before serving and cook for 30 seconds only.*

Herbal Shrimp

Serves 2 people: For lovers only

8 jumbo shrimp
½ teaspoon finely-chopped fresh chives
1 tablespoon finely-chopped fresh parsley
¼ teaspoon dry mustard
2 garlic cloves, peeled and cut into halves
⅛ teaspoon nutmeg
⅛ teaspoon black pepper
2 tablespoons dry white wine
1 tablespoon golden sherry
½ cup clarified butter
1 cup fine unseasoned breadcrumbs

1. Split the shrimp down the back of their shells. Remove the veins and carefully remove the meat without breaking the shells. Reserve the shells.
2. Marinate the shrimp for several hours in the chives, parsley, mustard, garlic, nutmeg, pepper, wine, and sherry.
3. Heat the butter over a medium fire and toss the shrimp until completely coated. Remove the shrimp and chop them into coarse pieces.
4. Stir the marinade into the butter. Bring to a boil for about ten seconds. Remove from the fire and cool.
5. Discard the garlic cloves. Fill the reserved shrimp shells. Set them into individual baking dishes and spoon a bit of the butter/marinade over each.
6. Toss the breadcrumbs into the remaining butter/marinade and cover each shrimp, patting the crumbs tightly across the tops of the shrimp.
7. Bake at 400° for 10 minutes. Decorate with artichoke hearts, tiny tomatoes, and parsley.

Shrimp Jambalaya

Serves 6 people

1 pound Andouille or smoked, spicy sausage, sliced thin
2 pounds raw medium-sized shrimp, shelled and deveined
Oil to cover the bottom of a large pot (bacon fat is marvelous)
2 onions, chopped coarse
1 green pepper, cut into thin strips
1 red pepper, cut into thin strips
1 yellow pepper, if available, cut into thin strips
1 teaspoon chili powder
1 tablespoon thyme
1 teaspoon ground oregano
2 bay leaves
3 cloves minced garlic
1 teaspoon hot Hungarian paprika
6 peeled and chopped tomatoes (Italian plum, if possible)
15-ounce can tomato bits or stewed tomatoes, chopped, with juice
3-ounce can tomato paste

1. Sauté onion, celery, pepper, and garlic until soft in the oil or fat. Stir in everything else except the sausage and shrimp and cook over a medium fire, uncovered, for 15 minutes. Taste for salt and pepper. (I never add salt to seafood, because it has enough natural salt.) Stir in the sausage and cook another 5 minutes.
2. Just before serving, stir in the shrimp, which have been shelled and deveined.

NOTE: *The sauce may be made a day or two in advance—or even frozen for the future. Make it without the shrimp and toss the shrimp in directly before serving. Serve with rice or pasta.*

This recipe is absolutely delicious. It is perfect for family or the most elegant company, as well as one of the easiest dinners to serve. A good mixed salad on the side provides you with a complete menu.

Shrimp Ke-bab

Serves 4 people

24 jumbo shrimp, shelled and deveined, with shells left on the tails
(10–12 to the pound)
2 cloves garlic, whole or cut in halves
1 diced onion
4 tablespoons chopped parsley
4 tablespoons soy sauce
4 tablespoons brown sugar
1 tablespoon powdered ginger
½ teaspoon dry mustard
½ cup olive oil
Juice of 1 lemon
2 tablespoons light sherry
24 whole water chestnuts

1. Combine all ingredients. Marinate shrimp several hours. Remove garlic cloves.
2. Put shrimp on skewers with green pepper, mushrooms, onion, and water chestnuts or put shrimp on skewers with fresh pineapple cubes, fresh melon cubes, large whole grapes, and water chestnuts.
3. Barbecue, grill, or broil, basting frequently until well done. Do not overcook. Serve with Rice Pilaf on page 162.

Shrimp Stuffed Lobster

Serves 4 people

4 Maine lobsters, 1½ pounds each
28 small shrimp
¼ pound butter
4 tablespoons finely-chopped parsley
1 piece finely-chopped celery
2 finely-chopped shallots
2 tablespoons Worcestershire sauce
Juice of 1 lemon
2 beaten eggs
2 tablespoons dry sherry
1 tablespoon cognac or brandy
1 cup fine white breadcrumbs
½ teaspoon salt
⅛ teaspoon black pepper

1. Split the lobsters in half. Remove the sac and the vein, keeping the tomally and roe (if any) in tact.
2. Melt butter in a skillet. Add parsley, celery, and shallots, and cook until soft. Add Worcestershire, sherry, cognac, salt, and pepper.
3. Add shrimp and toss for a few seconds in the mixture. Remove from heat.
4. Beat the eggs in a separate bowl and stir in the breadcrumbs. Add to the shrimp mixture.
5. Fill the open cavity of the lobsters, covering the tomally and roe.
6. Lay the lobsters onto a sided cookie sheet and brush well with melted butter. Lightly cover the stuffing with a piece of aluminum foil to keep the crumbs from burning. Bake at 350° for 15 minutes. Remove the foil and bake another 5 minutes.

Shrimp Dijon

Serves 4 people

24 large shrimp
½ lemon
4 tablespoons butter
2 tablespoons minced fresh parsley
1 tablespoon chopped chives or green part of scallions
1 teaspoon Dijon mustard
½ teaspoon white pepper
¼ teaspoon ground ginger
1 11-ounce can mandarin oranges, drained
½ pound green seedless grapes, peeled
¼ cup dry white wine
2 tablespoons orange or apricot liqueur (Grand Marnier, Triple Sec, Grand Passion, Pêcher Mignon)

1. Clean the shrimp and squeeze the juice of the lemon over, tossing them well.
2. Put the butter, parsley, mustard, chives, pepper, and ginger into a pan and add the shrimp. Sauté for 1 minute. Add the wine and the liqueur and toss the shrimp until just done. Remove the shrimp with a slotted spoon to a serving dish. Add the mandarin oranges to the gravy and the grapes and bring to a boil. Pour over the shrimp and serve.

Crab Stuffed Artichoke Hearts

Serves 4 people

12 large canned artichoke hearts
1½ cups picked-over white crabmeat
1 tablespoon lemon juice, freshly-squeezed
3 drops Worcestershire sauce
½ cup good mayonnaise
⅛ teaspoon dry mustard
1 teaspoon dill weed
¼ teaspoon dried chervil or fresh parsley

1. Gently spread the center of each artichoke heart open as far as possible without tearing it.
2. Mix the lemon juice, Worcestershire sauce, mayonnaise, mustard, dill, and chervil together. Carefully fold in the crabmeat.
3. Spoon as much crabmeat into the hearts as possible. Serve very cold on a plate garnished with watercress and olives with a spoonful of dressing over each heart.

Dressing

1 cup sour cream
½ cup mayonnaise
3 tablespoons tarragon vinegar
1 teaspoon grated lemon juice
1 teaspoon salt
Dash pepper
1 clove crushed garlic
Small handful of parsley
2 teaspoons capers
3 anchovy fillets
The green part of two spring scallions

1. Combine the sour cream and mayonnaise in a bowl. Put the rest of the ingredients into a blender and pulverize. Fold into the mayonnaise/cream and refrigerate until very cold.

Crabmeat in Phyllo Dough Triangles

Yields 12–16 triangles as a first course or 24 triangles as finger hors d'oeuvres

Phyllo dough: Can be found in most frozen food departments or
  specialty stores.
2 cups cooked lump crabmeat, or a combination of crabmeat and
  raw shrimp
4 tablespoons butter or margarine
4 tablespoons flour
2 cups cream
¼ teaspoon white pepper
½ teaspoon salt
1 teaspoon chopped dill weed
1 tablespoon chopped parsley
2 tablespoons chopped scallion greens
½ teaspoon lemon juice
1 tablespoon Ouzo liquor

1. Melt the butter. Stir in the flour and the cream and cook until
   thick and smooth. Add the rest of the ingredients, saving the
   seafood for last. Remove from the stove and cool to room
   temperature.
2. Open the phyllo dough and cut into 4 strips lengthwise. This
   recipe will use ½ package of phyllo dough.
3. Using 2 strips for each triangle for thickness, spoon 2 tablespoons or more of the seafood onto the strip as shown in the
   diagram below. Fold as you would a flag to create a triangle.
   Brush all over with melted butter and place on a cookie sheet.
   Refrigerate or freeze until ready to cook.
4. Bake in a 375° oven until dough is golden brown and crisp.
   (about 20 minutes). Serve on grape leaves or with sprigs of
   watercress and cherry tomatoes and Greek olives for garnish.

*NOTE: Phyllo dough should be thawed in the refrigerator overnight and removed
just before using for the best results. If it thaws at room temperature, the leaves
will stick to each other.*

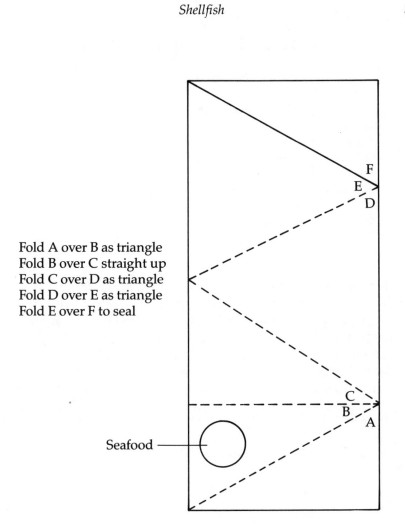

Fold A over B as triangle
Fold B over C straight up
Fold C over D as triangle
Fold D over E as triangle
Fold E over F to seal

Seafood

Avocado Filled with Scallops

Serves 4 people

1 pound bay scallops, whole, or sea scallops, cut up into quarters
2 ripe avocados
1 cup sour cream
¼ cup mayonnaise
2 tablespoons lime juice
1 tablespoon minced onion
1 teaspoon chili powder
½ teaspoon coriander
¼ teaspoon salt
Black pepper to taste

1. Marinate the scallops in lime juice for 1 hour.
2. Cut the avocados in half and remove the pit, leaving the skin on. Scoop out as much avocado from the skin as possible and mash it well. Mix in the rest of the ingredients (this may be done in a food processor) and fold in the scallops.
3. Heap the mixture into the avocado skins and sprinkle the tops with paprika. Serve very cold. A strip of pimento may be placed on top of each for decoration.

Scallops Provençale

Serves 2 people

1 pound scallops
Milk for dipping
Seasoned flour (salt-white pepper) for dredging
¼ pound butter for scallops
1 clove garlic
1 tablespoon minced fresh parsley
A little lemon juice
¼ cup white wine
¼ pound sliced mushrooms, sautéed in 1½ tablespoons butter

1. Dip the scallops into the milk and then into the flour. Put them into a shallow pan or dish and refrigerate for 1 hour.
2. Melt the butter for the mushrooms and sauté until done. Drain on absorbent paper and set aside.
3. Melt the butter for the scallops and add the parsley and garlic clove. Simmer for 5 minutes, and discard the garlic.
4. Turn the fire to medium and sauté the scallops on both sides until brown. Squeeze lemon over and toss.
5. Remove scallops with a slotted spoon to a heated platter. Pour in the wine and cook on high fire for 1 minute, stirring constantly. Pour over scallops and serve immediately.

Scallops with Tarragon

1 pound scallops (Cut into quarters, if large)
Drop of Tabasco sauce
2 slices lemon
2 teaspoons minced chives or scallion greens
1 teaspoon minced fresh parsley
¼ teaspoon minced dried tarragon or 1 teaspoon minced fresh
   tarragon
½ lemon
1 ounce clarified butter
½ ounce dry white sherry
1 ounce brandy

1. Pour butter into pan and add 1 drop Tabasco sauce. Add scallops and cook until almost done (about 30 seconds). Add parsley, chives, and tarragon.
2. Squeeze lemon juice over scallops. Season with salt and white pepper, if desired. Remove scallops with a slotted spoon to a chafing dish.
3. Add sherry and brandy to the pan. Bring to a boil and pour over the scallops, tossing them well in the mixture. Serve immediately.

Lobster Fra Diavolo

Serves 2 people: A complete dinner for lovers only!

2 (1½ pounds each) lobsters (preferably Maine)
2 cloves crushed garlic
1 small green pepper
2 large shallots
1 fresh tomato, skinned and chopped (Italian plum, if available)
2 15-ounce cans of Hunt's Tomato Sauce Special (or another brand
    of tomato sauce with bits of tomatoes, peppers, onions, and
    seasonings)
1 bay leaf
1 teaspoon powdered oregano
⅛ teaspoon black pepper
1 cup dry white wine
Pinch of crushed red pepper or 1 teaspoon hot Hungarian paprika
    (Optional)
Linguine or Angel Hair pasta for 2

1. Dice garlic, pepper, shallots, and tomato by hand. (Not in food processor)
2. Combine with the other ingredients (except the lobsters and the spaghetti) in a large roasting pan on top of the stove. (It will cover 2 burners.) Bring to a boil, stirring, and then turn to low. Cover and simmer for 1 hour or more. (May even be made 1 day in advance)
3. Split the live lobsters and remove the sac and vein to the tail. Take a small hammer and hit the claws just to crack in 2 places. Put the lobsters in the diavolo sauce meat side up. Bring to a boil, (turn on both burners), and spoon sauce over lavishly. Turn to low. Cover and simmer for 15 minutes.
4. While the lobsters are simmering, fill a soup pot with hot salted water and bring to a boil for the linguine or angel hair. Cook al dente.
5. Pile the pasta onto 2 plates and place the lobsters on top, spooning the sauce over lavishly. Serve immediately.

NOTE: I have suggested a thin pasta as the accompaniment to the lobsters because of the richness of the seafood. If your appetite is grander, choose another.

Poultry

Chicken Cacciatore

Pollastro Alla Cacciatore
Serves 8 people ¼ chicken each

2 chickens, cut into eighths
Salt and pepper
Flour for dredging
Italian olive oil or vegetable oil
4 whole cloves garlic
1 pound mushrooms, stems on, cut into halves
4 tablespoons butter
1 tablespoon minced fresh parsley
3 tablespoons flour
1 10-ounce can Campbell's Beef Broth Bouillon
2 coarsely-chopped large onions
4 fresh tomatoes, skinned and chopped (Italian Plum variety, if
    possible)
1 tablespoon finely-chopped fresh basil or 1 teaspoon dried basil
1 teaspoon powdered oregano, or 1 tablespoon minced fresh
    tarragon
2 green peppers, cut into strips
2 red peppers, cut into strips
2 yellow peppers, cut into strips (if available)
2 16-ounce cans stewed tomatoes and their juice

1. Salt and pepper the chicken pieces. Dust them with flour and
   set them aside.
2. Heat the oil and put the whole garlic cloves in to simmer on
   low for 10 minutes. Turn fire to high and brown the chicken
   pieces on both sides in the oil. Remove chicken pieces to a
   deep roasting pan. Discard the oil and garlic cloves.
3. In the same pan melt 4 tablespoons butter and sauté the
   mushrooms until soft. Stir in the parsley and the flour and the
   beef broth and cook a bit until thick and smooth. Stir in the rest
   of the ingredients and pour all over the chicken. If you're a
   garlic lover, crush 2 more cloves into the sauce.
4. Roast uncovered at 350° for 1 hour. Serve with the pasta of your
   choice.

*NOTE: "Cacciatore" means "The Hunter" in Italian. It always contains tomatoes
or tomato sauce.*
   This dinner is best when made in the morning or the day before.

Chicken Breasts Florentine

Serves 8 people

4 chicken breasts, cut into halves and pounded thin
4 eggs, beaten with 3 tablespoons water
2½ cups corn flour
1 teaspoon salt, 1 teaspoon white pepper, 2 tablespoons minced
    parsley
Vegetable oil to cover the bottom of a skillet plus 2 tablespoons
    butter
3 pounds fresh spinach (4 cups cooked)
½ cup butter
1 minced shallot
1 crushed garlic clove
1 teaspoon salt
½ teaspoon pepper
⅛ teaspoon rosemary
Juice of ½ lemon

1. Dip chicken breasts into the beaten eggs. Combine the corn
   flour with the salt, pepper, and parsley and dredge the chicken
   breasts.
2. Fry quickly in oil until brown on both sides and drain on paper
   toweling.
3. Steam the spinach and squeeze out all the water.
4. Melt the butter and sauté the shallot and the garlic with the
   rosemary over a very low fire for just a few minutes. Squeeze
   in the lemon. Add the salt and pepper and the spinach leaves
   and toss well. Cover the bottom of a greased, heatproof serving
   dish or casserole evenly with the spinach mixture.
5. Place the chicken breasts on top of the spinach in even rows
   and bake in a 350° oven for 20 minutes.
6. Directly before serving, spoon sauce over the chicken.

Sauce

2 tablespoons butter or margarine
2 tablespoons all purpose flour
1 cup strong chicken broth
½ cup white wine

1. Melt the butter and stir in the flour. Slowly stir in the chicken broth and cook until thick and creamy. Add the wine and continue to cook for five minutes.

NOTE: Any recipe with the word "Florentine" in its title includes spinach as one of the ingredients.

Chicken à la King

3 cups cooked chicken or turkey, cubed or in thin strips
2 tablespoons butter
3 tablespoons flour, all purpose
1 cup warm milk
1 cup warm heavy cream
¼ cup dry sherry
½ teaspoon salt
½ teaspoon white pepper
2 tablespoons pimento strips
Pinch of nutmeg
½ pound sliced mushrooms

1. Melt butter. Add the flour and stir in the warm milk and cream slowly, stirring with a wooden spoon and smoothing with a wire whisk until thick. Stir in the sherry and pimento strips.
2. Sauté the mushrooms in a little butter until soft and spoon them into the other mixture without their juice.
3. Add the chicken and taste for salt and pepper. Serve with cooked peas over toast points or patty shells. You can also fill large Cream Puffs (page 237).

NOTE: This is the original French Chicken à la King served throughout France.

Chicken Breasts Stuffed with Sausage

Marvelous for a crowd!

4 chicken breasts, boned and halved, but *not* skinned
½ cup butter or margarine
1 red pepper, chopped fine
1 small green pepper, chopped fine
1 large onion, or 3 large shallots, chopped fine
½ pound mild Italian sausage, cooked and crumbled in food
   processor
1 egg, beaten
½ cup commercial seasoned Italian breadcrumbs
Seasoned Italian breadcrumbs for dredging
4 eggs, beaten with ½ cup water
Vegetable oil for frying. Use just enough to cover the bottom of
   a skillet.

1. Arrange chicken breasts on wax paper for preparation.
2. Melt butter and sauté vegetables until soft. Stir in cooked
   sausage. Remove from fire.
3. Beat egg in a bowl and stir in vegetables. Stir in breadcrumbs. If
   too moist, add more crumbs just to bind.
4. Spoon a bit of the mixture directly under the skin of each
   breast, pushing it flat and covering it over completely with the
   skin.
5. Cover each breast first with crumbs and then dip in the egg/
   water mixture and once again in the crumbs. Set the breasts
   onto a cookie sheet covered with wax paper and refrigerate for
   1 hour. Fry on side with the pan covered. Remove cover and
   fry on the other side (about 6–8 minutes on each side). Remove
   to a heatproof platter or shallow casserole. Serve or set aside
   for later. These steps may be done in the morning or even the
   day before for a large crowd.
6. To reheat: Bake uncovered in the oven at 350° until very hot.

NOTE: *For a different flavor, eliminate the egg and use ¼ cup tomato paste
instead. Grate 1 tablespoon Parmesan cheese into the stuffing. Sausage stuffing
may be replaced with spinach or rice of your choice. These also freeze beautifully
to give you a company dinner the easy way.*

Chicken in Champagne

Serves 2 people: For lovers only

1 chicken, cut in half
½ teaspoon finely chopped savory
½ teaspoon finely chopped rosemary
1 teaspoon finely chopped chives
1 teaspoon finely chopped fresh parsley
1½ cups champagne
Salt and pepper
3 tablespoons peanut oil (or, to cover the bottom of a skillet)
¼ cup melted butter or margarine (4 tablespoons)
Flour for dredging
Large skillet with a cover

1. Combine the savory, rosemary, chives and parsley.
2. Lightly salt and pepper the chicken on both sides.
3. Dip the chicken into the melted butter, coating it all over.
4. Rub the herbs all over the chicken on both sides.
5. Dredge chicken lightly with flour, shaking off the excess. (The old trick of putting flour into a sandwich bag and shaking the chicken in it is still the best.)
6. Heat the oil over a high fire until bubbly. Turn the fire to medium-high and brown the chicken on both sides.
7. Slowly pour in the champagne. Cover the skillet and cook the chicken, skin side up, over medium-high for 35 minutes, or until tender. Check to make sure the fire is not too hot and chicken is not sticking to the bottom of the pan. Add a bit more champagne if liquid absorbs. Reduce heat to medium the last 15 minutes.
8. Pour gravy over chicken and serve with sautéed endive and glazed carrots, and tiny whole red potatoes.

NOTE: Gravy will thicken as it cooks. If you don't have champagne, make chicken the poor man's way: 1 cup white wine mixed with ½ cup unsalted seltzer water for the same effect.

Chicken Française and Tarragon

Serves 6 people

3 chicken breasts, skinned, boned and halved
2 cups breadcrumbs
3 eggs, beaten with 4 tablespoons water
¼ cup butter
1 cup cooking oil

1. Sprinkle chicken breasts with salt and pepper.
2. Season bread crumbs with a little white pepper.
3. Dip the chicken breasts first into the crumbs, then into the egg, and dredge well with the crumbs. Refrigerate on a cookie sheet for 1 hour.
4. Sauté the chicken, covered, in butter/oil mixture. Dry on paper toweling and transfer to an ovenproof dish or casserole to keep warm in the oven.
5. Serve with Sauce Française or Tarragon.

Sauce Française

2 tablespoons butter
2 tablespoons flour
1 10-ounce can concentrated chicken broth
½ cup dry white wine
Juice of ½ lemon

1. Melt butter and stir in flour. Slowly add chicken broth, wine, and lemon juice, stirring until thick and smooth.

Sauce Tarragon

2 tablespoons butter
1 tablespoon minced shallots
1 tablespoon flour
1 cup dry, white wine
1 teaspoon dried tarragon, or 2 teaspoons chopped fresh tarragon
¾ cup heavy cream

1. Sauté the shallots in the butter until soft. Stir in the flour and the wine and cook until thick and smooth. Stir in the tarragon. Just before serving, stir in the heavy cream.

Chicken Stuffed with Ham

Serves 4 people

1 3-pound chicken
¼ pound baked ham
2 tablespoons grated Parmesan cheese
1 egg
1 teaspoon ground sage, or 2 fresh minced sage leaves
1 teaspoon ground rosemary, or 4–5 sprigs fresh rosemary
2 tablespoons brandy
Salt and pepper
2 tablespoons olive oil
1 cup chicken broth
Paprika

1. Chop the ham fine and combine it with the cheese, egg, sage, rosemary, and brandy. Stuff the chicken at both ends with this mixture.
2. Sprinkle the chicken all over the outside with salt and pepper and place breastside down in a roasting pan with the chicken broth. Sprinkle with paprika. Brush all over with olive oil.
3. Roast 1 hour at 375°. Turn it over and roast another 30 minutes, or longer, until crisp.
4. Serve with tiny pearl onions, which have been steamed and glazed in a small bit of white wine.

Fried Chicken

2 fryers, cut into 8ths
Salt and black pepper
4 cups bread flour
1 tablespoon poultry seasoning (Spice Islands or McCormick)
2 eggs
⅔ cup buttermilk
Vegetable oil

1. Mix the poultry seasoning into the flour.
2. Combine the eggs and milk and beat with a fork.
3. Salt and pepper the chicken all over, rubbing the seasoning in with your hands.
4. Dredge the chicken first in the flour. Shake off excess. Dip in the buttermilk mixture and then dredge well again in the flour.
5. Pour vegetable oil ½" deep into a heavy skillet and bring to the boiling point.
6. Place the chicken in the oil, reducing the heat to medium-high when the pan is full. Cover and cook until very brown on one side. Remove cover. Turn chicken and cook, uncovered, until very brown on the other side. Remove chicken pieces to paper toweling to drain.

NOTE: I could never make decent fried chicken until a friend from Georgia gave me this simple recipe. It's crunchy on the outside and juicy on the inside.

Chocolate Chicken Wings

For the kinky

24 chicken wings, drumsticks separated from wings: wing tips
   discarded or used for gravy or stock.
1 tablespoon allspice
1 teaspoon cinnamon
1 teaspoon salt
1 teaspon garlic powder
2 tablespoons Grand Marnier
¼ cup orange juice

1. Rub marinade well into chicken wings. Dredge wings in flour.
Fry in vegetable oil until brown and crisp. Remove to an
ovenproof serving dish.

½ cup finely-chopped orange peel
½ cup julienned candied ginger (Paradise or Dromedary type for
   fruitcakes)
¼ teaspoon nutmeg
2 tablespoons brown sugar
2 tablespoons white sugar
2 cups orange juice
½ cup Grand Marnier or Triple Sec
1¼ cups white wine
3 teaspoons cornstarch
1 ounce unsweetened chocolate

1. Combine the above in a saucepan. Bring to a boil, stirring, until
thick and smooth. Turn fire to simmer and cook for ten minutes, stirring often. Cool.
2. Reheat wings in a 350° oven for 15 minutes. Heat the sauce and
pour over the wings or serve separately as a dipping sauce.

Chinese Chestnut Chicken and Pork

2 chicken breasts from a 4–5 pound chicken
1 pound lean pork shoulder
¼ cup sesame oil
1 clove crushed garlic
1 tablespoon sugar
⅓ cup soy sauce
1 pound chestnuts, whole, peeled, and, if possible, fresh
4 chinese black mushrooms, soaked in boiling water 10 minutes
    and sliced thin
1 whole star anise (ba-kock), chopped coarse
1" piece of fresh green ginger
4 tablespoons Port wine
¾ cup water

1. Cut chicken and pork into strips 1½" long and about ⅛" wide.
2. Heat the oil with the garlic and sauté the pork and chicken over a medium fire for a few minutes, or until the chicken is done.
3. Add the sugar, soy sauce, chestnuts, mushrooms, ba-kock, ginger, wine, and water. Cover and cook over a very low fire for 30 minutes. Serve over rice which has been browned in a little soy sauce before cooking.

Garlic Chicken

Serves 2 people

1 broiler chicken, cut in half
½ cup vegetable or peanut oil
4 cloves garlic, chopped coarse
2 shallots, chopped coarse
1 piece celery, chopped fine
½ teaspoon rosemary
1¼ cups rich beef broth

1. Sauté the vegetables and rosemary in the oil until soft.
2. Salt and pepper chicken and add to pan. Add broth and spoon over chicken. Cover and cook for 45 minutes.
3. Remove cover and place chicken under broiler until brown.

Cornish Hens

Serves 4 people

4 Cornish game hens
Salt and pepper
1 cup light sherry
3" piece of fresh ginger
2 garlic cloves
1 cup white wine
1 cup water
¼ teaspoon dried chervil
¼ teaspoon dried thyme
6 Porcini dried Italian mushrooms, soaked in boiling water for 10
   minutes

1. Salt and pepper the hens. Chop the mushrooms and combine
   them with the rest of the ingredients. Pour over and roast,
   uncovered, at 350° for 1 hour.

*NOTE: Put slivers of fresh ginger and garlic into a bottle of sherry and keep it in
the refrigerator to use wth poultry, seafood, or pork.*

*Cornish hens are good with a variety of stuffings. One of my favorites for this
recipe is my Rice and Dried Mushrooms on page 160.*

Stuffed Roast Squab with Pâté

Serves 2 people

2 whole squabs
Salt, pepper, paprika
½ cup water
¼ cup Scotch whiskey
2 tablespoons butter, softened

1. Stuff the squabs with pâté stuffing after washing and drying the cavity.
2. Lightly salt and pepper the squabs and sprinkle them with paprika. Place them in a small roasting pan breastside down.
3. Pour the water and the Scotch over and rub the squab well with the butter. Roast, uncovered, at 325° for 1 hour, basting frequently.
4. Serve with glazed sweet potatoes or sweet potato stuffing on the side.

Pâté Stuffing

2 tablespoons butter
Hearts, gizzards, livers from the squabs
½ cup raw ground loin of pork
1 minced shallot
⅛ teaspoon nutmeg
1 tablespoon finely-chopped carrot
1 tablespoon brandy or cognac
⅛ teaspoon black pepper
¼ teaspoon salt
1 truffle or 4 pitted black olives, finely-chopped

1. Melt butter and sauté pork, carrot, shallot, nutmeg, gizzards, livers, and hearts for 5 minutes. Add brandy and sauté 5 minutes longer. Cool and pulverize in a food processor. Stir in the truffle pieces.
2. Stuff the squabs.

NOTE: *You may prepare the stuffing in advance but do not stuff the squabs until immediately before roasting.*

Roast Squab with Polenta

Serves 4 people

4 whole squabs
Salt and pepper
⅛ teaspoon each sage, thyme, and minced onion for each squab
2 apples (Rome, Jonathan, or Granny Smith)
6 tablespoons butter or margarine
½ cup water
4 slices bacon
4 pieces Polenta

1. Lightly salt and pepper the outside of the squabs. Mix the sage, thyme, and onion together and rub well into the cavities.
2. Peel and chop the apples and stuff the squabs.
3. Brush all over with melted butter or margarine and bake breast side down in a roasting pan at 325° for 40 minutes, basting every 15 minutes.
4. Remove and wrap each squab with a whole strip of bacon, securing it with a toothpick underneath.
5. Bake another 7–10 minutes, or until the bacon is crisp.
6. Serve on top of the Polenta.

Polenta

6½ cups water
1 tablespoon salt
1¾ cups yellow corn meal

1. Bring the water and salt to a rolling boil in a large pot.
2. Turn the fire down to medium-high and slowly pour the corn-meal into the water, stirring constantly with a wooden spoon. Reduce the fire to simmer and cook for at least 20 minutes, or until very thick.
3. Spoon onto a cookie sheet, or into a shallow baking pan, and refrigerate for at least 2 hours. Slice into large squares and fry in vegetable oil until crusty on both sides. Drain on paper towels.

NOTE: Polenta may also be sliced and broiled or baked at 400° until crisp. Polenta slices should be ½" thick.

The Secret of Good Duckling

1. Have the butcher cut the duck in half and cut off the backbone.
2. Cut off all excess fat and slash the skin and fat underneath to the meat in a criss-cross fashion, creating a basketweave design all over.
3. Put the duckling halves into a large shallow pan or disposable aluminum roaster, skin-side up. Salt the skin heavily and put into a very hot 500° oven, uncovered. Cook for ½ hour and pour off the amazing amount of fat from the pan.
4. Combine 1 tablespoon flour with 4 cups white wine and stir until blended. Add ¼ cup brandy. This will be enough to baste three ducks (6 halves).
5. Pour the flour/wine/brandy mixture over the duck halves and bake, uncovered, in a 350° oven, for 2½ hours, basting every 20 minutes. If mixture becomes too thick, stir in more wine.
6. When duckling is done, remove it from the pan and discard any gravy from the bottom. Serve with your favorite sauce.

NOTE: *Duckling is the easiest of all the gourmet dinners because it can be made in the morning or the day before and reheated. Serve with the Wild Rice Ring (page 163) and a green vegetable.*

Sauces for Duckling

Bing Cherry Sauce

1 16-ounce can pitted Bing cherries
1 cup red Dubonnet or Port wine
½ teaspoon ground cloves
½ teaspoon ground ginger
½ cup black currant jelly
1 teaspoon arrowroot

1. Combine the juice from the cherries, the Dubonnet, cloves, ginger, and currant jelly in a saucepan and bring to a boil, stirring. Turn fire to low, add the arrowroot and the cherries and stir until thickened.

Framboise Sauce

1 pint fresh raspberries
1 10-ounce package frozen raspberries
½ cup Kirschwasser
¼ cup Chambord liqueur
1 teaspoon arrowroot

1. Defrost the frozen berries. Force them with their juice through a sieve or fine strainer to remove seeds. Put the strained liquid into a saucepan with the Kirschwasser, Chambord and bring to a boil, stirring. Turn fire to low, add the arrowroot and stir until thickened. Surround the cooked duckling with fresh raspberries and pour the sauce over all.

Mango, Peach, or Apricot Sauce

6 peaches or 12 small apricots or 2 mangoes
1 cup apricot jam
½ cup apricot juice
For Mango Sauce: ½ cup light Rum
For Peach Sauce: ½ cup Pêcher Mignon or Peach liqueur
For Apricot Sauce: ½ cup Apricot liqueur
⅔ cup almonds, blanched and slivered
1 teaspoon lemon juice
1 teaspoon arrowroot

1. Poach the peaches or apricots for 10 seconds and remove their skins under cold, running water. Cut them into halves and remove the pits.
2. Combine the jam, juice, liqueur, and lemon juice in a small saucepan and bring to a boil. Add the almonds. Reduce the heat to low and stir in the arrowroot.
3. Just before serving, stir in the apricots or peaches or peeled and sliced mangoes.

Duck and Pasta Salad

16 ounces of a combination of interesting pasta such as shells
   or fuselli
2 quarts water
2 whole garlic cloves, peeled
1" slice fresh green ginger
2 teaspoons salt
1 teaspoon black pepper
1 ounce olive oil
¼ cup Italian olive oil

1. Combine all ingredients except the pasta and boil for 5 minutes. Stir in pasta and cook until not quite done. Pour off all water and drain in a colander, but do not rinse. Pour ¼ cup Italian olive oil through and mix well with two spoons.

1 cooked duckling, skin removed, chopped into small pieces
1 small green pepper, chopped coarsely
1 sweet yellow or red pepper, chopped coarsely
1 teaspoon powdered ginger
4-ounce bottle of green pimento olives, sliced
1 cup sliced water chestnuts
4-ounce can of pitted black olives, cut into halves
3 tablespoons soy sauce
Black pepper to taste

2. Combine the above with the pasta and taste. Add more soy sauce or black pepper or salt to taste. Refrigerate for several hours. Serve over Romaine lettuce.

NOTE: *Three whole chicken breasts may be substituted for the duckling. This is a perfect recipe for leftover duckling.*
  Six cups cooked rice may be substituted for the pasta.

Beef

Bassano Beef

Serves 8 people

4 pounds bottom round beef
Salt and pepper
2 fresh tomatoes, peeled and diced
1 large chopped Bermuda onion
2 fresh minced basil leaves, or, 1 tablespoon dried basil
Several minced oregano leaves or 1 tablespoon dried oregano
4 cups Burgundy wine (1 bottle)
4 large potatoes, cut into quarters, skins on
6 chopped carrots
2 tablespoons tomato paste

1. Salt and pepper the beef. Put into a large stew pot (or slow cooking crockpot) with the wine, basil, oregano, onion, and diced tomatoes. Bring to a boil and then reduce heat to medium-high and cook for 2½ hours, covered. (If using a crockpot, cook slowly for 4–6 hours.)
2. Add the potatoes and carrots and continue to cook for another 45 minutes, or until done.
3. Remove beef, potatoes and carrots to a deep serving dish. Allow to cool and slice the beef thin. Stir the tomato paste into the pot and bring to a boil. Pour gravy over the beef. Decorate with miniature cooked zucchini and cherry tomatoes. Serve with a good salad on the side and fresh bread.

NOTE: May be cooked and left in its gravy overnight for a better flavor. Slice cold before reheating.

Beef Steak Pie, Beef and Kidney Pie, and Beef and Oyster Pie

2 pounds boneless chuck, cut into 2" cubes
½ pound veal kidneys, cores removed, washed in cold water
1 teaspoon salt
½ teaspoon black pepper
1 cup flour
1 large onion, chopped
Dash of Worcestershire sauce
1 tablespoon chopped fresh parsley
1 whole bay leaf
1½ cups rich beef broth
3 tablespoons dry sherry

1. Cut the kidneys into small pieces and blanche in boiling water for five minutes.
2. Dredge the beef cubes in the flour, which has been seasoned with the salt and pepper, and brown it quickly on a medium-high fire on all sides in enough butter, margarine, or bacon fat combined with vegetable oil to just cover the bottom of a heavy deep skillet.
3. Add the onion and allow it to brown with the beef. Add Worcestershire sauce, parsley, bay leaf, beef broth and 1 cup hot water and stir until blended. Cover and simmer for 1½ hours, or until the meat is tender. Check the gravy as the meat is cooking to make sure it is not too thick, and add more water or beef broth to thin to the desired consistency.
4. Add drained kidneys. Add sherry and stir. Allow to cool slightly.
5. Put the beef and kidneys in a deep pie dish, mounding it higher in the center than the outer edges so it will have an abundant look. Cover with the following crust:

Crust for Pie

2 cups all-purpose flour
½ teaspoon baking powder
½ teaspoon salt
½ cup shortening (cold butter or solid vegetable shortening or lard)
⅓ cup ice water

1. Sift baking powder, salt and flour into a bowl. Cut or mix shortening into it, blending together quickly. Add ice water until mixture sticks together easily but is neither wet nor dry. It may take a little more or less than ⅓ cup water. Form into a ball and cover with wax paper. Refrigerate for 1 hour.
2. Roll out until it is larger than the pie plate. Fit over the top of the meat and seal the edges well over the pie plate with ice water. Brush with 1 egg yolk which has been beaten with 2 tablespoons milk. Prick the crust in several places for air to escape, and bake at 450° for 20 minutes, or until the pastry has risen and is brown. Lower heat to 350° and bake 15 minutes more. Serves 4–5 people.

For Oyster and Beef Pie

Same as above, but substitute 2 dozen oysters for the kidneys. Blanche the oysters in their own liquor for 5 minutes. Cool. Strain. Reserve for use in the pie.

Delicious and Easy Filet of Beef – For Lovers Only

Tournedos

2 filets, cut 1½" thick
2 tablespoons unsalted butter or margarine
¼ pound sliced mushrooms
½ cup chili sauce
¼ cup Worcestershire sauce
2 tablespoons butter
2 tablespoons Madeira wine or sweet sherry

1. Melt 2 tablespoons butter and sauté the mushrooms until soft. Stir in the chili sauce and the Worcestershire sauce. Set aside. This may be done in advance.
2. Lightly salt and pepper the filets. Melt 2 tablespoons butter in a small pan and sauté the fillets quickly on both sides. Pour the sherry over and continue to cook until desired doneness.
3. Spoon the mushroom sauce over and stir to combine.

NOTE: Cook your vegetable and potato in advance and arrange attractively on a heatproof platter in the oven. Set the fillets in the center and serve immediately.

Beef Stroganoff

Serves 4 people

2 pounds filet of beef
2 large shallots, minced
1 clove garlic, minced (not crushed)
½ pound mushrooms, or more, sliced thick
6 tablespoons unsalted butter
3 tablespoons flour
2 10-ounce cans Campbell's Beef Broth Bouillon, or 2½ cups
  homemade broth
3 tablespoons ketchup
¼ cup Port wine
⅛ cup brandy
1 bay leaf
1 teaspoon dried chervil, or, 2 teaspoons minced fresh parsley
6 tablespoons salted butter
½ cup sour cream
1 pint small boiler onions, left whole, pre-boiled and skinned
6 ounces wide egg noodles

1. Boil the onions. Remove the skins and reserve.
2. Sauté the shallots, garlic, and mushrooms in the unsalted butter until soft. Stir in the flour and the beef broth, slowly, until thickened. Add the ketchup, wine, brandy, bay leaf, and chervil, and stir, bringing all to a boil. Reduce heat to medium. Cover the skillet and simmer for 45 minutes. Turn off the fire.
3. Boil the noodles al dente and rinse with hot water through a colander.
4. Heat the butter. Cut the filet into bite-sized cubes or strips 1" thick and lightly salt and pepper them. Quickly sear them in the hot butter leaving the insides very rare. Stir the meat into the gravy and bring it almost to a boil. Remove pan from the stove and stir in the sour cream.
5. Portion the noodles onto 4 plates. Cover with the stroganoff and spoon the onions over the top of each.

NOTE: Steps 1 and 2 can be done in advance, but in order for the Stroganoff to be truly delicious, the last 3 steps must be done at the last minute. This can be accomplished by bringing the cooked noodles to the table and cooking the beef over a réchaud (hotplate or burner) in front of your company.

Brisket (Breast) of Beef

Good old-fashioned eating

1 whole well-trimmed brisket
Salt, black pepper, onion powder
2 large chopped onions
2 whole cloves
1 bay leaf
2 tablespoons ketchup
1 teaspoon powdered allspice
Water and rich beef broth (canned is fine) in equal parts just to
   cover meat
3 tablespoons flour
½ cup cold water

1. Season brisket all over with salt, pepper, and onion powder. (If you are a garlic lover, sprinkle a small amount of powdered garlic over the meat.) Smooth the seasonings into the meat with your fingers. Wrap in foil and put into the refrigerator overnight or for several hours.
2. Place into a deep roaster and add the onions, cloves, bay leaf, ketchup, allspice, water and beef broth. Cover the roaster and place into a 350° oven for 3 hours. (The weight of the meat doesn't make any difference. Three hours cooks any brisket perfectly.)
3. Remove from the oven and cool completely. Refrigerate until very cold and remove the fat which will congeal at the top. Slice while cold by cutting across the grain from the smallest corner.
4. Mix the flour and water together and stir into the cold gravy. Return the sliced brisket to the pan (or serving casserole dish) and heat at 350° for 15 minutes before serving.
5. Serve potato pancakes and homemade applesauce on the side. Yummy!

Corned Beef Hash

Brunch or Dinner

2½ cups finely-chopped cooked lean corned beef
4 medium-sized potatoes, peeled and boiled
1 finely-chopped Bermuda onion
1 small finely-chopped green pepper
2 tablespoons minced parsley
¼ cup ketchup

1. Chop by hand or in a food processor all the above ingredients, reserving the ketchup. Pour into a bowl and add the ketchup.
2. Mix well together with hands and shape into round balls. Flatten slightly into patties.
3. Heat a stickproof skillet over medium-high and cook the patties, covered, until brown on one side. Turn them over and cook, covered, until brown on the other. (Covering will steam the patties so the onion will cook inside.) If they brown too fast, turn the fire lower. Serve with or without fried or poached eggs with ketchup on the side.

NOTE: *If you don't have a stickproof skillet, barely cover the bottom of a regular skillet with vegetable oil.*

The hash may also be put into a shallow greased 8" square pan instead of forming patties. Bake at 400° for ½ hour, or until very brown on top. Cut into squares.

Cocktail balls for hors d'oeuvre may also be made, following the same instructions. Bake the balls at 400° on a cookie sheet until brown. Serve with toothpicks for a unique hors d'oeuvre.

Filet of Beef en Croûte or Wellington

¼ cup red wine
½ cup olive oil
2 teaspoons black pepper
2 teaspoons salt
1 tablespoon Worcestershire sauce
1 large crushed garlic clove
1 large onion
Handful of parsley
1 whole, well-trimmed filet of beef tenderloin

1. Put the first 8 ingredients in a blender. Pour over the filet and turn it several times to cover with the marinade. Marinate overnight in the refrigerator tightly covered.
2. Remove from the marinade and pat dry with paper toweling.
3. Sear quickly without oil in a non-stick frying pan or on a griddle, turning on all sides until very dark.
4. Place on a cookie sheet in a preheated 250° oven for 20 minutes. Reduce heat to 200° and bake another 20 minutes. Remove from oven and cool completely. (This method of cooking the whole filet was made famous by James Boggess from Miami for *The March of Dimes Gourmet Gala*. The filet emerges red but now raw. It is a foolproof technique.)

Make Quick Puff Pastry as Follows

2 cups sifted, all-purpose flour
½ teaspoon baking powder
½ teaspoon salt
½ pound butter less 2 tablespoons (14 tablespoons total), cold and cut into pieces.
½ cup ice water

1. Put the flour, baking powder, butter, and salt into a food processor and turn on/off quickly three times. (Or, combine with a pastry blender or fork until mealy.)
2. Remove to a bowl and pour the water in a little at a time, working quickly with your hands. Form into a ball and then flatten slightly.

3. Roll out to a 12″ × 6″ rectangle on a floured surface. Fold into thirds. (Top third of rectangle over center, bottom third over the top) to create a rectangle approximately 6″ × 4″. Roll out again. Fold into thirds again. Roll out to approximately ¼″ thickness. Set the filet on top.

For Wellington

1. Spread a heavy layer of pâté de foie gras across the top of the filet.
2. Fold the dough around the beef, cutting off any excess from the ends. Seal the edges and flap which you have overlapped slightly with ice water.
4. Place onto a coated or greased cookie sheet flap side down. Beat 1 egg yolk with 1 tablespoon milk and brush the top and sides. If you have any dough left over, roll it out and cut hearts or other shapes with a cookie cutter, and place them on top in a design. Brush them with the egg wash. Refrigerate until ready for the final cooking.
5. Preheat oven to 400°. Remove filet from refrigerator and bake for 25–30 minutes, or, until very brown. Serve immediately surrounded by a variety of green and yellow vegetables for color.

NOTE: *The colder the pastry when it is placed into the oven, the lighter it will be. Also, the meat will remain rare inside when it is cold.*

CHEATERS' NOTE: *If you don't have time or inclination to make your own puff pastry, buy the frozen. (Pepperidge Farm makes an excellent brand.) You will need 2 boxes, or 4 sheets, which can be rolled into 1 piece.*

Gravy for Filet

2 tablespoons butter
1 large minced shallot
1 tablespoon minced parsley
4 dried mushrooms, soaked for 10 minutes in hot water
2 tablespoons flour
1 tablespoon beef extract (specialty food stores)
2½ cups rich beef bouillon
½ cup red Dubonnet

1. Melt butter in a saucepan and sauté the shallot, parsley, and chopped mushrooms over a low fire until soft.
2. Stir in the flour and the beef extract and immediately stir in the bouillon and wine, stirring with a wire whisk until thick and smooth. Serve as an accompaniment to any beef.

Shish Ke-bab

Serves 4 people

2 pounds boneless sirloin, or top round first cut, or lamb cubes, cut into 1″ squares
Juice of 2 lemons
4 tablespoons Italian olive oil
½ teaspoon crushed garlic, 1 teaspoon cumin powder, 1 teaspoon coriander powder, 1 teaspoon ginger powder, and 2 teaspoons chili powder
3 teaspoons salt
¼ teaspoon black pepper
¾ cup canned or homemade rich chicken broth
24 cherry tomatoes
2 large green peppers, cut into ½″ squares
2 large red peppers (fresh), cut into ½″ squares
24 pearl onions, peeled
24 mushrooms, cleaned and left whole

1. Combine meat, lemon juice, oil, seasonings and chicken broth. Marinate meat cubes for at least 1 hour in this mixture.
2. Put meat on skewers, alternating with the vegetables.
3. Broil or barbecue until done, basting frequently.

NOTE: To peel onions: Drop into boiling water for 15 seconds. Rinse under cool water. Cut off root at bottom and slip off skin. Serve with Rice Pilaf (page 162).

Stuffed Cabbage

2 cups cooked white rice
1 large onion
1½ pounds lean ground beef
1 egg
½ teaspoon salt
¼ teaspoon pepper
1 large (curly leaf is best) green cabbage
28 ounce can tomatoes in tomato paste
12 ounce can tomato paste
2 bay leaves
6 tablespoons brown sugar
1½ teaspoons sour salt
2 garlic cloves, crushed
1 teaspoon ground ginger

1. Cook the rice. Cool to room temperature.
2. Cut up the onion and put it in a blender with the egg. Blend on high speed until pulverized. Combine onion/egg, ground meat, rice, salt and pepper and work well with the hands.
3. Carefully remove leaves from the cabbage by first cutting a circle around the top and removing the hard core. Use as many leaves as possible, saving the center for cole slaw.
4. Plunge the leaves individually into boiling water for no more than ten seconds just to soften them. Shake off any excess water and remove any hard core left which keeps the leaves from bending easily.
5. Put about 2 tablespoons of the meat mixture in the center of each leaf and fold the edges over in a square. Secure each with a toothpick and place in a baking dish.
6. Pulverize the tomatoes in the blender and combine with the tomato paste, bay leaves, brown sugar, sour salt, ginger, and garlic. Bring to a boil in a saucepan, stirring, and allow to simmer for 5 minutes. Pour over the cabbage.
7. Bake at 325° for 1 hour, covered. Serve in the same baking dish over a flame.

NOTE: *Make the day before and reheat at 300° for ½ hour. The flavor settles overnight.*

Oxtail Ragoût

Serves 4 people

3 pounds well-trimmed beef oxtails
½ cup vegetable oil
Flour for dredging, salt and black pepper
1 clove crushed garlic
1 bay leaf
1 cup Burgundy wine
2 cups concentrated beef broth
1 diced green pepper
1 diced large onion
4 tablespoons tomato paste
1 tablespoon minced parsley
1 cup tomatoes, chopped coarse. (or 1 16-ounce can)
¼ cup Porcini dried mushrooms, soaked in hot water for 10
    minutes

1. Season the oxtails lightly with salt and pepper. Dredge them in flour. Put enough vegetable oil in a large roaster to cover the bottom and heat to the bubbly stage over a burner. Brown the pieces quickly in the oil on all sides and remove them to paper toweling.
2. Sauté the onions, green pepper, and garlic in the same oil over a low fire until soft. Drain off as much of the oil as possible and put the tomatoes, mushrooms, bay leaf, tomato paste, parsley, wine, and beef broth into the roaster. Bring to a boil, stirring. Add the oxtails, spooning the sauce over well. Cover until very tender. Cool and refrigerate overnight.
3. One hour before serving, take the oxtails from the refrigerator and remove all the fatty crust from the top. Place in a 300° oven, covered.
4. Peel about 8 large carrots. Slice thick on a slant with a serrated cutter, and boil until tender.
5. Wash as many small red potatoes as you wish, leaving the skins on, and boil until tender.
6. Spoon oxtails and gravy into a large serving dish and cover the top with the carrots and potatoes.

NOTE: *Serve with a French or Italian roll to dip into the gravy.*

Bratwurst

8' natural casing (can be purchased from butcher shops)
1 tablespoon white vinegar
4 cups ice water
3 beaten eggs
1 cup fine breadcrumbs
1½ cups cold seltzer or ice water
2 pounds pork shoulder
1 pound veal shoulder
½ pound bacon
½ teaspoon nutmeg
1 tablespoon marjoram
2 cloves crushed garlic
1 tablespoon caraway seeds
2 teaspoons salt
1½ teaspoons pepper

1. Open the end of the casing and fit it around the water spout in the sink. Slowly fill with cool water as far as possible before cutting. Continue filling until all the casing has been washed inside and out. Combine the vinegar with the ice water and soak the casing while preparing the filling.
2. Combine beaten egg, seltzer, and breadcrumbs and allow to stand until soft and thick.
3. Cut the pork, veal, and bacon into cubes and put into the food processor with the nutmeg, marjoram, crushed garlic, caraway seeds, salt, and pepper. Pulverize fine.
4. Put mixtures 1 and 2 together and mix until well-blended.
5. Remove the casing from the water and pat dry on paper toweling. Push the mixture into the casing with a piping bag fitted with a large round tip. (Or, if you have one, use the stuffing horn attachment of your mixer.) Make each sausage about 3"–4" long, leaving approximately ¼" casing loose on each end. Tie off or twirl up the ends, and cut them as close to the sausage as possible.
6. When all have been made, freeze or refrigerate until ready for use.

7. Brush with butter or bacon fat and broil, fry, or grill until just done and lightly browned.

NOTE: *You may never want to buy sausage again after tasting your own homemade. This is a take-off on the traditional one made by every German housewife. (With, of course, no exact measurements.)*

Steak Stuffed with Onions and Peppers

For lovers only

2 rib-eye steaks cut ¾" thick
1 chopped shallot
1 clove crushed garlic
1 finely-chopped red or green pepper
Olive oil
Butter
Black pepper

1. Slice through the centers of the steaks creating a "pocket."
2. Sauté the shallot, garlic, and pepper in a little butter or margarine until very soft. Drain off the butter.
3. Spoon the mixture into the pockets and close each steak with a wooden or steel skewer. Sprinkle the outside of the steaks very well with black pepper and brush all over with olive oil. Allow to marinate for several hours in the refrigerator.
4. Cook quickly over a very hot barbecue or grill.

NOTE: *This is an incredibly easy recipe, which is one of the most flavorful meat dishes you have ever tasted. The seasoning of the steak from the inside gives a new meaning to beef. It's actually a dish you can order in any "Osteria" (Truck Stop eatery three grades lower than a Trattoria, which is a grade lower than a Ristorante) on the road in northern Italy.*

Steak Valerie

For lovers only

2 ¾" steaks, cut from the tenderloin, strip, or rib
2 tablespoons clarified butter
2 tablespoons minced shallots
4 large mushrooms, sliced thick, or quartered
¼ teaspoon garlic powder, or 1 small crushed garlic clove
Juice of ½ lemon
1 teaspoon dry mustard
1 teaspoon thyme
1 tablespoon chopped parsley
Dash of Worcestershire sauce
2 ounces heavy cream (measure with a "shot" glass)
2 sprigs parsley, for garnish

1. Melt the butter in a small pan and sauté the mushrooms with the garlic until just soft. Stir in the lemon, mustard, thyme, parsley, and Worcestershire sauce and simmer for 1 minute. Set aside.
2. Sprinkle pepper all over the steaks and brush lightly with oil. Broil or grill quickly on both sides and set on a serving dish or individual plates.
3. Reheat sauce to the boiling point. Remove from the fire and stir in the cream quickly. Serve immediately.

Note: This is a combination of Steak au Poivre and Steak Diane.

Veal

Veal with Asparagus and Cheese

Serves 4 people

8 asparagus spears
4 veal escallops, pounded thin
Salt and freshly ground pepper
¼ cup fine breadcrumbs
¼ pound butter
½ pound thinly-sliced fresh mushrooms
4 thin slices Provolone cheese
Juice of 1 lemon

1. Cook the asparagus quickly in rapidly boiling water in a covered skillet for about 2 minutes. Remove from the water and set aside.
2. Sprinkle the veal with salt and pepper and coat with breadcrumbs. Refrigerate for ½ hour.
3. Heat 2 tablespoons butter and sauté the mushrooms until golden brown.
4. Heat 2 tablespoons of the butter in a large skillet and sauté the veal until brown on both sides.
5. Place the veal slices in a row on a heatproof dish. Sprinkle each piece with mushrooms. Arrange asparagus spears on top of each slice of veal. Cover each with a piece of cheese. Place under a hot broiler until brown and bubbly.
6. Melt the rest of the butter and add the lemon juice. Pour over the veal. Garnish with watercress and baby tomatoes.

Veal with Crab and Asparagus

Serves 4 people

The Topping

8 large white asparagus spears
4 large pieces Alaskan King crab claw meat

The Sauce

10 ounces clarified butter
4 egg yolks
Juice of ½ lemon
¼ teaspoon salt
⅛ teaspoon white pepper

1. Clarify the butter and heat until bubbly.
2. Place yolks into a blender and turn on high for 2 seconds. Pour in the lemon juice, salt, and pepper, and turn on low for 2 seconds. Turn the blender on low and *very* slowly pour in the butter in a steady stream until the mixture is thick.

The Veal

4 2-ounce veal escallops, pounded thin
Salt, pepper, flour
2 tablespoons dry white wine
1 minced shallot
¼ teaspoon tarragon

1. Salt and pepper the veal lightly on both sides and dust with flour.
2. Fry the veal quickly on both sides in enough unsalted butter to cover the bottom of the pan. Remove from the pan and set onto a warm platter.
3. Deglaze the pan by pouring in two tablespoons dry, white wine, and bringing it to a boil, stirring constantly until the wine, butter, and flour bits left from the veal are blended.

4. Stir in the minced shallot and tarragon and cook over a low fire for 5 minutes. Strain the sauce into the top of a double boiler and stir in the sauce from the blender. Stir for a minute over simmering water and spoon over the veal escallops. Top each escallop with the crabmeat and garnish with the asparagus spears.

NOTE: *This is a rich dinner dish and should be accompanied by a light salad with a lemon base dressing.*

Veal Fontina

Serves 8 people

8 veal escallops, pounded thin
⅓ cup cream
¼ pound finely-chopped Fontina cheese
3 black olives, chopped
½ cup Westphalian ham or Prociutto, cut into strips
1 beaten egg

1. Sauté veal quickly on both sides in a little unsalted butter. Remove to a shallow baking dish that is pretty enough to bring to the table.
2. Heat cream and cheese together, stirring constantly over a low fire until cheese is melted. Add olives and ham. Remove from the heat. Add a bit to the beaten egg before stirring the egg into it.
3. Spoon over veal and set the broiler until bubbly. Serve at once with 16 tiny unpeeled whole red potatoes, which have been roasted in a shallow pan with bouillon.

Veal Chausseur

Serves 4 people

4 escallops of veal, pounded thin
2 tablespoons oil
1 cup combination of diced carrots, onion, and celery
1 tablespoon flour
1½ cups concentrated beef broth bouillon
1 tablespoon minced parsley
1 bay leaf
Salt and pepper
2 tablespoons tomato paste
1 tablespoon oil
2 minced shallots
½ pound thinly-sliced mushrooms
½ cup dry white wine

1. Sauté the carrots, onion, and celery in oil over low heat just until soft. Stir in flour, beef broth, parsley, bay leaf, salt, pepper, and tomato paste.
2. Sauté the shallots in 1 tablespoon oil. Add the mushrooms and sauté until done. Stir in the wine and bring to a boil.
3. Combine the 2 sauces and keep warm.
4. Cut tiny slits around the outside edges of the veal to keep them from curling during the cooking. Dip them into beaten egg. (Add one tablespoon water with each beaten egg.) Dredge in fine bread crumbs. Sauté quickly on both sides in enough butter just to cover the bottom of the pan.
5. Remove veal slices to a serving platter and spoon the sauce over them. Garnish with parsley and lemon.

NOTE: "Chausseur" means "The Hunter" in French. Whenever you see a recipe with the word "Chausseur," it includes tomato sauce.

Stuffed Breast of Veal

6 pound, or larger, veal breast, well-trimmed of all fat with
   "pocket" for stuffing
⅛ teaspoon pepper
1 cup Worcestershire sauce
1 large minced onion
1 minced green pepper
1 minced sweet red pepper
1 minced tomato
1 crushed garlic clove
⅓ cup olive oil
2 cups rice
Pinch saffron
¼ teaspoon dried basil, or 2 fresh leaves, minced
4½ cups water
1 6-ounce can tomato paste
1 pound Italian mild sausage, precooked, drained, and crumbled

1. Sprinkle both sides of veal heavily with salt and pepper and rub in the Worcestershire sauce. Marinate for at least 2 hours.
2. Sauté onion, peppers, tomato, and garlic in the olive oil until tender. Add rice and toss with 2 spoons until completely coated. Add saffron and stir. Add water. Stir. Bring to a boil. Stir again and cover. Turn to low. Cook for ½ hour. Add tomato paste and sausage. Stuff veal pocket as full as possible. (It will hold more than it looks.)
3. Place veal, fat side up in a large roasting pan. Cover the bottom with water. Add one cup of dry white wine and cook, uncovered, for 2½ hours at 350°.

Veal Picatta

Serves 4 people

8 thin veal escallops
1 cup dry breadcrumbs seasoned with a bit of salt, white pepper, and parsley
3 eggs, beaten with 3 tablespoons water
Vegetable oil to just cover the bottom of a skillet

1. Dip the veal escallops into the egg and then into the breadcrumbs, tapping any excess crumbs off. Refrigerate for 1 hour.
2. Remove veal from refrigerator and sauté quickly on both sides. Remove to a heatproof platter in a 150° oven while you make the following sauce:

Sauce

1 pound thinly-sliced mushrooms
4 tablespoons butter
⅛ teaspoon nutmeg
1 teaspoon flour
4 tablespoons beef broth
¼ cup white Italian wine
2 tablespoons chopped parsley
1 tablespoon brandy

1. Sauté the mushrooms in the butter until soft. Add the nutmeg and the flour and stir into the mushrooms. Slowly add the beef broth, parsley, and wine, and continue stirring and cooking until the sauce has thickened.
2. Heat the brandy in a steel measuring cup. Light a match to it and, as it flames, stir it into the sauce. Pour over the veal and sprinkle freshly-chopped parsley heavily over the top. Garnish with lemon slices and surround with hot tomatoes stuffed with small green peas and finely-chopped ham.

Veal Piquante

Serves 6 people

6 rib veal chops, cut ¾" thick
4 tablespoons butter
¼ cup dried mushrooms, soaked in hot water for 15 minutes,
    drained, and chopped
¼ cup chopped sweet red pepper
2 tablespoons chopped spring green scallion stems
6 spring green onion bulbs
1 tablespoon chopped parsley
12 medium-sized mushrooms
1 tablespoon flour
½ cup dry white wine
½ cup chicken broth

Vegetables

1. Melt butter in a skillet and sauté the vegetables until soft.
2. Sprinkle the flour over the vegetables and stir in the wine and chicken broth very slowly over a low fire until blended. Leave on simmer while cooking veal.

Veal

1. Salt and pepper the veal on both sides. Heat 4 tablespoons butter with 2 tablespoons olive oil in a skillet and sauté quickly on both sides. Remove to a serving dish and spoon the vegetables over.

NOTE: Serve with tiny "elbow" macaroni on the same plate or whole parsleyed potatoes.

Blanche's Rib Veal Chops

Serves 2 people

2 rib veal chops, bone left in, cut ¾" thick
½ cup matzo meal combined with ½ cup fine breadcrumbs
1 egg, beaten with 1 tablespoon water
Salt and pepper
Vegetable oil, just to cover the bottom of a skillet

1. Lightly salt and pepper veal chops on both sides. Sprinkle a little salt and pepper into the matzo meal/breadcrumb mixture.
2. Beat the eggs with the water.
3. Dip the chops into the matzo meal mixture, then into the eggs, and then into the matzo meal mixture again. Place on a plate or wax paper and refrigerate about ½ hour, or until very cold.
4. Heat the oil to the sizzling point and fry the chops on both sides until brown and crisp, but still slightly pink in the center. Drain on paper toweling. Serve immediately with applesauce or salad.

Viennese Veal

Follow the instructions for Blanche's Veal Chops, or double the recipe for 4 people. Serve with 4 tablespoons Demi-Glace Sauce (page 107) for each chop and put a lemon slice on top with capers, hard boiled eggs, or black caviar. Serve with zucchini bundles and tiny whole red boiled potatoes or Rice Pilaf on the side. Tomatoes stuffed with seasoned breadcrumbs are pretty and good with this.

VARIATION: Viennese Veal does not have to be breaded and fried when served with the demi-glace sauce. Brush each chop with olive oil and place on the barbecue (with hickory chips or mesquite, if possible) to brown on both sides.

NOTE: Good veal chops should be bought from an Italian or Jewish-style butcher shop. They are more expensive, but better quality.

Rolled Veal Stuffed with Spinach

Serves 6 people

1 large piece of veal rump, about 1¾ pounds, butterflied to about
   ¼" thickness
1 cup cooked and chopped fresh spinach
3 slices cooked bacon
1 large beaten egg
2 tablespoons grated Parmesan cheese
2 tablespoons melted butter
Salt and pepper
½ cup dry white wine
¼ cup chicken broth

1. Have the butcher butterfly a large veal rump. If it is too thick to
   roll, either have the butcher pound it thin; or put the meat
   between two pieces of wax paper and pound it to ¼" thickness
   yourself.
2. Cook the spinach in a tiny bit of water, covered, over a high fire
   for only 3 minutes, or until soft but still green. Cool, drain, and
   squeeze *all* the water out. Put it into a bowl and chop fine.
3. Cook the bacon until done but not crisp. Cut it into small
   pieces. Add it to the spinach. Stir in the beaten egg and the
   cheese.
4. Spread the filling lengthwise down the center of the veal and
   roll up as tightly as possible. Tie up with string. Place flap side
   down onto a shallow baking pan. Salt and pepper the veal and
   brush with melted butter. Pour the wine and broth over and
   cook at 325° for 30 minutes. Serve with the bacon strips, or
   crumbled bacon, across the top, interspersed with chopped
   parsley.

NOTE: Meat will actually not "roll," but will "flap" over.

Veal for Vitello Tonnato

Tonnato Under Tuscan Tuna

4 pound loin of veal (Have the butcher bone a rib roast and keep
   the bones)
1 large onion
2 stalks celery
1 clove garlic
Salt, pepper
1 cup white wine
1 cup chicken broth or veal stock

1. Cut the onion, celery and garlic into large pieces and place in
the bottom of a shallow baking pan. Sprinkle the veal with salt
and pepper and add to the pan on top of the vegetables.
2. Roast it in a 400° preheated oven 15 minutes. Add the wine and
stock, reduce the heat to 325° and roast 1 hour, basting every
20 minutes. Let the veal cool in the liquid. Drain off the liquid
when cool and save for gravy for another time. Refrigerate the
veal until very cold.
3. Slice veal very thin and put back together as though whole.
Make Tuscan Tuna and spread it lavishly over the top and
sides, allowing it to cover the area directly around the veal.
Decorate the platter with parsley, anchovies, sliced hard boiled
eggs, capers, and a few cherry tomatoes or strips of fresh red
pepper. Refrigerate until ready to serve.

*NOTE: This is a beautiful buffet item for either luncheon or dinner, and mar-
velous for the summertime. It may be prepared a day in advance and decorated
before serving.*

Demi-Glace Sauce

The hard way!

10 pounds veal bones, with some meat attached
8 carrots, cut coarse
4 medium onions
1 whole stalk celery, with leaves
10 whole black peppercorns
2 bay leaves
3 large whole cloves garlic
2 chopped shallots
2 teaspoons dried thyme
2 gallons water
1 bunch parsley leaves
2 15-ounce cans whole tomatoes, drained

1. Preheat the oven to 400°.
2. Put the bones into a large, sided cookie sheet or roasting pan. Bake 2 hours, turning the bones every ½ hour. Put the carrots, onions, and chopped celery over the top of the bones and bake another ½ hour.
3. Transfer the bones and vegetables to a large soup pot. Add a bit of water to the cookie sheet and scrape up all the brown particles which are adhering to it, putting them into the soup pot. Add the rest of the ingredients. Bring to a boil and simmer over very low heat for 8 hours. (Skim the top often at the beginning.) Cool.
4. Strain into small containers. This sauce will keep for several weeks in the refrigerator and months in the freezer.
   WHEN READY TO USE: Thaw to cold liquid stage. For each cup liquid melt 1 tablespoon butter and stir in 1 tablespoon flour. Stir in 1 ounce tomato paste and 2 tablespoons brandy. Stir until boiling and thick.

Sautéed Kidneys

Serves 4 people

1 pound veal kidneys
½ pound mushrooms
1 tablespoon butter
½ teaspoon salt
½ teaspoon white pepper

1. Clean and slice mushrooms thick and sauté in the butter until soft. Season with salt and pepper and set aside.
2. Remove fat and veins from the kidneys and cut into slices. Put into water to cover and bring to a boil. Boil for 3 minutes and drain off water. Rinse well under cold water.

2 tablespoons butter
1 tablespoon flour
½ cup beef broth
2 tablespoons Madeira or Port wine
½ cup cream

1. Heat butter in a skillet and sauté the kidneys until lightly browned on both sides. Add mushrooms with their liquid.
2. Sprinkle the flour evenly over and stir well. Slowly stir in the broth and wine until thickened. Stir in cream and cook over a low fire until very hot but not boiling. Serve over toast points with boiled potatoes or buttered noodles.

Lamb

Curried Lamb or Veal

2½ pounds shoulder of veal or lamb, cut into 1" cubes
3 onions, chopped fine
1 whole bay leaf
2 cloves finely-chopped garlic
1 teaspoon thyme
1 teaspoon marjoram
1 teaspoon salt
½ teaspoon black pepper
2 cups water
2 tablespoons curry powder
1 pint coffee cream, or half cream, half milk

1. Cut the meat into 1" squares.
2. Chop the onions and garlic fine and combine with the thyme, marjoram, salt, pepper, meat and water in a skillet. Bring to a boil, cover, and cook over medium-high heat for 45 minutes, or until very tender and the water has evaporated. Turn the fire to very low.
3. Slowly stir in the cream, incorporating it with the flavors of the veal. Sprinkle the curry powder over and stir until well-blended. Serve immediately over rice or broad noodles.

NOTE: This needs no thickening agent. I love this dish because the flavor is mild and subtle. It is marvelous to serve company. Remove from the fire after step #2 and stir in the cream and curry while the company wait.

Indonesian Lamb

Serves 6 people

4 pound leg or shoulder of lamb
1 cup dry red wine
2 tablespoons minced onion
2 cloves crushed garlic
1 teaspoon ground coriander
½ teaspoon cayenne pepper
⅛ teaspoon saffron
8 tablespoons olive oil
1 tablespoon powdered ginger, or a 1″ piece of fresh ginger

1. Marinate the lamb in the above ingredients overnight in the refrigerator by wrapping tightly in foil.
2. Place on a rack in a roasting pan and roast in a 350° oven for 1½ hours, basting frequently.
3. Serve with rice and chutney.

Leg of Lamb Provençale

5–5½ pounds cooking weight boned, whole leg of lamb
Salt and pepper
1 tablespoon dried rosemary; or 6–8 sprigs fresh rosemary
1 teaspoon dried savory; or, 6 sprigs fresh savory
2 large cloves garlic; or 4 medium cloves (do not use powdered)
1 cup red bordeaux wine
1 whole branch of mint leaves about 12″ long. (There is no
    substitute for fresh mint. You can make this lamb without it and
    it will be good, but the fresh mint makes it marvelous.)
2 tablespoons olive oil for brushing

1. Have the butcher bone a leg of lamb and trim off almost all the fat. Salt and pepper the lamb all over lightly.
2. Set the mint branch on the bottom of a small deep roaster. Sliver the garlic cloves and put several slivers and a few sprigs of the rosemary and savory along the bottom of the lamb. Place the lamb fat side up in the roaster.

3. Cut shallow slits along the top of the lamb and insert the slivers of garlic. Put the remaining rosemary and savory all along the top and brush with the olive oil.
4. Pour the wine into the bottom of the roaster and brush the lamb with it. Marinate, covered, several hours.
5. Add 1 cup water to the roaster and roast, uncovered, for 20 minutes at 500°. Reduce heat to 350° and cover. Roast about 1 hour more.
6. Remove lamb to a serving platter. Skim off as much fat as possible from the pan and pour ¼ cup mint sauce into the gravy. Strain the gravy over the lamb and serve.

Mint Sauce for Lamb Provençale

10 fresh mint leaves
½ cup water
¾ cup sugar
1 cup apple jelly

1. Put the mint leaves and the water into a blender and blend on high speed until leaves are minced. Put into a saucepan with the sugar and boil hard for 8 minutes, stirring around the edges with a wooden spoon to remove mint leaves, which adhere to the sides.
2. Cool until ready for use. Stir in apple jelly with a wire whisk. Serve on the side as a separate gravy garnished with fresh mint leaves.

Lamb Parisian

Serves 8 people

1 whole leg or shoulder of lamb
4 cloves minced garlic
Salt and pepper
1 whole bay leaf
1 teaspoon marjoram
¼ teaspoon minced thyme
½ tablespoon minced parsley
3 tablespoons olive oil
1 minced onion
1¼ cup concentrated beef broth (1 10-ounce can)
Juice of 1 lemon
6 slices thick bacon

1. Remove almost all fat from the lamb. Set lamb into a small, deep roaster and sprinkle salt and pepper all over. Rub the onion, thyme, parsley, and garlic all over.
2. Brush with olive oil.
3. Put the bay leaf in the bottom of the roaster with the beef broth, and squeeze in the lemon. Baste the lamb with this mixture, and allow to marinate at least 1 hour.
4. Preheat the oven to 500° and roast the lamb, uncovered, fat side up, for 20 minutes. Reduce heat to 350°, place the bacon strips across the top of the lamb and cover. Roast for 20 minutes per pound.

Stuffed Crown Roast of Lamb

Serves 4 people

1 whole rack of lamb
¼ cup olive oil
⅛ cup Worcestershire sauce
1 garlic clove, crushed

1. Have the butcher chime and feather the bones, trim fat, and slice in-between each bone to turn the lamb rack into a "crown" or circle tied up together. Salt and pepper the lamb lightly and rub the above marinade all over and into the openings. Refrigerate overnight.
2. Cover the chop tips with foil so they won't burn during the cooking.
3. Put into a shallow pan and bake at 325° for 1 hour 15 minutes until perfectly pink.

Stuffing

½ pound shoulder of lamb, diced into small squares
½ cup diced celery
1 small bunch diced scallions, greens and bulbs
1 tablespoon diced fresh parsley
1 can water chestnuts, sliced thin
2 cups raw brown rice
1 teaspoon salt
½ teaspoon black pepper
1 teaspoon tumeric powder
½ teaspoon chili powder
2½ cups water
2½ cups rich chicken broth

1. Sauté celery and onions in ¼ pound butter until soft in a pot.
2. Stir in the rice and toss until well-coated.
3. Add the rest of the ingredients and bring to a boil. Stir once, and cover. Turn fire to low and cook slowly for about 20 minutes, or until liquid is absorbed. Pile the stuffing into the center of the lamb, sprinkle with freshly-chopped parsley and serve.

Jalapeño Mint Crown Roast of Lamb

Your company will "clean the bones"

1 whole rack of lamb
2 crushed garlic cloves
1 teaspoon salt
½ cup olive oil
½ cup Jalapeño mint jelly (found in specialty food stores)
Fresh mint sprigs

1. Have the butcher chime and feather bones and slice in-between each bone to turn the lamb rack into a "crown" or circle tied up together.
2. Combine the oil, salt, and crushed garlic and rub all over and into the roast. Cover tightly and refrigerate overnight.
3. One hour before cooking remove lamb from refrigerator and rub the Jalapeño mint jelly all over and into the lamb between the cracked bones.
4. Roast in a pre-heated 325° oven for 1 hour 15 minutes. It will be slightly pink for a perfect feast.

NOTE: This is truly "King's Eating" and my favorite banquet for special people. I fill the inside of the crown with Rice Pilaf (page 162) topped with fresh pine nuts and fresh mint sprigs and surround the roast with sliced fresh Kiwi fruit and poached peach halves filled with raspberries. Julienned zucchini poached for just a minute in a little butter and a squeeze of fresh lime tops off this magnificent presentation.

Liver

Barbecued Liver Steaks

Liver, 1" thick, short slices
Black pepper
Flour for dusting
1 large onion
2 tablespoons unsalted butter
½ cup dry white wine
¼ teaspoon thyme

1. Season liver with pepper and dust with flour. Brush the barbecue grill with oil so liver will not stick.
2. *ONION COVERING:* Cut onion on the round very thick. Cover the bottom of a fry pan with water and steam the onion until it becomes limp. Remove the cover and allow the water to evaporate. When the water has evaporated, put 2 tablespoons butter into the pan and cook the onion, stirring occasionally, until it turns golden but not burned. Pour wine over, stirring, and add the thyme. Set aside to wait for liver to be barbecued.
3. Barbecue liver until charred on each side, but still raw in the middle, turning the liver steaks with a spatula instead of a fork so as not to puncture.
4. Remove liver to a shallow baking dish and cover with the onion mixture described above. Put into a preheated 400° oven until done (generally about 5 minutes). Be careful not to overcook. Liver continues to cook even after being removed from the heat, and overcooked liver is unpalatable.
5. Serve immediately with a piece of cooked bacon on top of each liver steak.

Whole Braised Calf's Liver

2 pound piece of calf's liver, left whole
2 teaspoons salt
¼ teaspoon white pepper
1½ tablespoons unsalted butter
1½ cups rich bouillon
½ ounce Scotch whiskey

1. Trim, wash and wipe the liver. Rub with salt and pepper. Sear in the butter in a heavy skillet until evenly browned, turning with tongs or wooden spoons (do not puncture with a fork).
2. Add bouillon and Scotch and cook slowly, covered, for 30 minutes, basting occasionally.
3. Remove from skillet to a heatproof platter and keep warm.

Gravy

2 tablespoons butter
2½ tablespoons flour
1 cups pan juice
½ cup heavy cream
Salt, pepper

1. Strain pan juices and reserve. Melt butter and add flour, stirring until blended. Stir in pan juices. Simmer 10 minutes, stirring occasionally. Stir in cream. Season to taste.
2. Slice liver thin and pour sauce over. Garnish with chopped parsley. Serve with boiled potatoes and fresh spinach.

Liver Marinara

Serves 3 hungry or 6 not-so-hungry people

6 thin slices liver ⅓" thick
Flour for dredging
2 tablespoons Italian olive oil
1 large diced green pepper
1 large diced onion
½ pound sliced mushrooms
1 clove crushed garlic
1 tablespoon chopped parsley
½ teaspoon oregano
½ cup dry white wine
1 cup chopped canned tomatoes and their juice
1 pound sweet Italian sausage, precooked in a 400° oven in foil,
   drained, and cut into 1" pieces
2 tablespoons tomato paste

1. Sauté the vegetables and spices in a few tablespoons butter until soft.
2. Add tomatoes and juice and the wine and bring to a boil, stirring. Add the sausage. Remove from the heat.
3. Dredge the liver in flour and fry quickly in hot oil on both sides until brown but not tough. Remove the slices to a warm serving dish and cover with the sauce. Serve immediately.

Sautéed Calf's Liver

Serves 1 Person

1 medium onion, sliced thin
Flour for dusting liver
1 piece liver, cut at least 1" thick
2 tablespoons butter
¼ teaspoon thyme or tarragon (thyme gives a tangy taste; tarragon
   is slightly sweet—take your choice)
1 teaspoon freshly-chopped parsley
Salt and pepper
4 tablespoons dry white wine (Chablis)

1. Steam onion in a little water in the same pan you will later
   sauté the liver. Remove to a dish for later.
2. Pour off water and melt the butter.
3. Dust the liver with flour and sauté with parsley and thyme or
   tarragon over a medium-high to high fire until crisp and brown
   on both sides. Add the onion and cook until brown. Sprinkle
   with salt and pepper and add the wine. Cook in the wine until
   desired doneness. (Just a minute or two will produce perfect
   rare liver.) Serve immediately.

Pork

Crown Roast of Pork with Apple Stuffing

Serves 8–12 people

12 pork ribs, cut from the center cut rib end
1 clove garlic
Salt, pepper, and lemon juice
2 medium onions, chopped into small cubes
2 pieces celery, chopped into small cubes
1 teaspoon minced parsley
⅛ teaspoon nutmeg
½ teaspoon cinnamon
2 tablespoons white sugar
2 large, tart apples, peeled and chopped into small cubes
½ cup peanut or soy oil
1 cup dried bread cubes
¼ cup boiling water

1. Have the butcher chime and remove the feather bone and form the pork chops into a crown, cutting the bones every chop for easy cutting later.
2. Rub the roast well with the garlic clove and sprinkle with salt, pepper, and lemon juice.
3. Combine onions, celery, parsley, nutmeg, cinnamon, sugar, and apples, and sauté for a few minutes in the oil until the apples are soft.
4. Add the bread cubes and the boiling water and mix well.
5. Fill the "crown," piling the stuffing as high as possible. Cover the stuffing and bones with foil. Bake at 350° for 2½ hours in 1 cup white wine mixed with one cup chicken broth and 2 cups canned whole cranberries.
6. Remove foil. Put paper "panties" on the tops of each rib and serve surrounded by apple rings, which have been carefully sautéed in butter.

Pork and Chicken with Mushrooms

Serves 4 people

1 cup raw pork, cut into strips (½ pound)
1 cup raw chicken, cut into strips (⅓ pound)
4–5 dried mushrooms
3 tablespoons peanut oil
2 cloves garlic
2 tablespoons light dry sherry
1 teaspoon soy sauce
¼ cup ginger preserves
1 cup canned water chesnuts (8-ounce can)

1. Soak the mushrooms in hot water for 15 minutes. Pour off water and slice into pieces.
2. Heat the peanut oil and simmer the garlic cloves in it for 10 minutes. Add the chicken and the pork and cook slowly until done. Discard the garlic cloves and stir in the sherry and soy sauce. Stir in the ginger preserves and the water chestnuts.
3. Serve over rice or pasta with the following gravy:

Gravy

½ cup rich chicken broth (made by boiling the chicken bones with 2 cups water)
1 tablespoon oyster sauce
½ teaspoon sugar
2 teaspoons cornstarch (dissolved in 2 tablespoons cold water)

Pork Roast with Rosemary

1 5-rib boned pork loin
4 sprigs fresh rosemary, or ¼ teaspoon dried
⅓ cup Jerez sherry, or American port
1 tablespoon apricot preserves
1 teaspoon Dijon mustard
1 clove crushed garlic or ¼ teaspoon garlic powder
2 tablespoons chopped spring onion greens
1 teaspoon cornstarch

1. Marinate the pork in the above ingredients for 1 hour, after stirring them together well.
2. Put into a small pan and roast at 350° for 1½ hours, uncovered, basting every half hour.
3. Slice thin and serve on a platter with gravy on the side.

Sweet and Sour Spareribs

2 pounds Canadian back ribs or very lean pork ribs
1 large minced onion
2 minced green peppers
2 strips minced bacon
¼ cup ginger marmalade
1 small can crushed pineapple in its own juice
½ cup firmly-packed brown sugar
¼ cup vinegar
2 tablespoons soy sauce
1 teaspoon cornstarch
¼ cup Kirschwasser brandy

1. Combine onion, green pepper, and bacon in a pan and cook over a very low fire until soft.
2. Add the canned pineapple and its juice, brown sugar, vinegar, and soy sauce. Dissolve the cornstarch in the cold water and stir in. Cook, covered, for about 5 minutes.
3. Pour the sauce over the ribs and marinate for several hours.
4. Bake the ribs in the oven at 375° in a cookie sheet with sides (jellyroll pan) for 45 minutes to 1 hour, basting frequently, or grill over charcoal until brown and finish in the oven.

NOTE: *If you use regular pork ribs, boil them first for 20 minutes before marinating to tenderize.*
This sauce is also delicious with chicken wings.

Ham

The best ham comes from the leg of the pork. The shoulder is also used, but is less delicate. The salting and smoking of pork to produce ham is of French origin. It was the Gauls, who first became known for the salting, smoking, and curing of pork. This was because France, at that time, was covered with huge forests in which the herds of pigs wandered. The role of the ham and all forms of salt pork has been so important in France that a special Ham Fair is held yearly in Paris during the three days preceeding Good Friday. This is called the Foire du Lard, (The Bacon Fair) and has been held since the 1700s.

The finest French ham is the Jambon de Bayonne, and is eaten raw as an hors d'oeuvre or with breakfast. The York, or English ham, is a salted ham, and should be boiled before glazing. It may be served with a wine sauce or a sweet glaze. The Mainz ham is the most popular of Germany, and is eaten raw. The best known "prosciutto," or raw, smoked ham of Italy is the Parma ham. (Parma is best known for its cheese, where the name "Parmesan" comes from.) It is truly a delicacy, and the Italians pride themselves on serving the finest ham in the world because of the way it is smoked. They eat it for breakfast, lunch, dinner, and as a snack in-between meals as a quick "pick-up." The best known Spanish ham is the Asturias. It is a mild-tasting, delicate ham, which is boiled.

The sweet ham may be accompanied by the same vegetables, sweet potatoes, and jello molds as the Thanksgiving turkey. The salt-cured ham, or baked with spices, is better with boiled parsley potatoes, green vegetables, and salad. The boiled ham is excellent in sandwiches and salads, and the smoked ham is delicious all by itself, sliced thin on rolls as a sandwich, or as an hors d'oeuvre or with breakfast.

To Boil: Bring water to a boil before adding ham. Cover and boil gently 25 minutes per pound.

To Bake: Bake covered at 325°—30 minutes per pound.

Buffet Ham En Croûte

12–14 pound smoked ham, boned and rolled (about 8 pounds after
  bone is removed)
2 cups golden rum
2 cups brown sugar
1 tablespoon Dijon mustard
1 6-ounce can unsweetened pineapple juice
2 tablespoons Worcestshire sauce
1 large onion, minced
1 bay leaf

1. Combine the above ingredients and pour over ham. Bake,
   covered, in a large roaster for 1 hour at 350°, basting every 15
   minutes. Uncover and cook another ½ hour, continuing to
   baste. Cool in the gravy.
2. Wrap in quick puff pastry. Brush with egg wash (1 egg beaten
   with 2 tablespoons milk), and bake at 375° on a cookie sheet for
   40 minutes, or until brown and puffed. Serve with sauce on the
   side. Decorate the platter with fresh pineapple and kumquats.

Sauce

½ cup golden rum
½ cup each: orange marmalade, ginger marmalade
3 tablespoons yellow mustard
2 cups dark brown sugar
1 cup light brown sugar
1 6-ounce can unsweetened pineapple juice
1 ounce Grand Marnier liqueur
⅛ teaspoon ground cloves
1 orange (do not remove rind) sliced thin
½ lemon (do not remove rind) sliced thin

1. Bring all the ingredients to a boil in a saucepan and simmer for
   a minute or two. Serve in a sauceboat.

Country Ham

12-14 pound raw whole leg of pork
½ cup Coca Cola
½ cup bourbon
2 tablespoons dark karo (corn) syrup
2 teaspoons ground cinnamon
2 teaspoons ground cloves
½ teaspoon ground nutmeg
2 16 ounce boxes light brown sugar (4 cups)
½ cup Coca Cola
½ cup bourbon

1. Remove most of the fat from the pork leg and salt and pepper it lightly. Place into a shallow roasting pan. Combine ½ cup Coca Cola with ½ cup bourbon and pour it over pork leg, turning to saturate well on all sides.
2. Make a paste with the rest of the ingredients and rub half all over the pork. Reserve the other half. Cover the pork and refrigerate overnight.
3. Preheat the oven to 325°. Set the pork on a rack and pour the rest of the paste over the top. Roast, uncovered, 20 minutes to the pound, or approximately 4 hours. Baste after the first hour only.
4. Cool completely. Remove the solidified fat from the gravy. Slice the pork thin and pour the remaining gravy over. Serve warm or at room temperature with Chutney (page 168) on the side.

Vegetables

Broccoli Mold

½ pound sliced mushrooms
1 finely-chopped onion
4 cups broccoli stems (about 4 stalks)
½ lemon
1 package frozen green peas
3 tablespoons butter
3 tablespoons flour
½ cup milk
½ cup cream
1 teaspoon tarragon
½ teaspoon salt
½ teaspoon white pepper
¼ pound grated sharp cheddar cheese

1. Sauté mushrooms and onion in a small pan and set aside.
2. Cook broccoli stems in a small amount of water until very tender. Squeeze the juice of the lemon over. Put into the food processor with the uncooked peas and pulverize.
3. Melt butter. Add flour. Stir in milk and cream until thickened. Add seasonings and cheese and continue stirring until smooth. Stir in sautéed mushrooms. Add pulverized broccoli and peas. Spoon into an oiled ring mold and place it in a pan of water in the oven.
4. Bake at 350° for ½ hour, covered with foil.
5. Cook broccoli flowerettes in a small amount of water, covered, until tender but still crisp and green (about 5 minutes).
6. Unmold the broccoli onto a platter, filling the center and surrounding with the flowerettes.

Asparagus Filled Artichoke Bottoms

Serves 12 people

12 large artichoke bottoms, cooked
1 pound fresh asparagus
2 minced shallots
6 tablespoons butter
Pinch of salt, black pepper, and grated nutmeg
1 level teaspoon Summer Savory
Juice from ½ lemon
1 small potato, boiled until very soft

1. Melt the butter and sauté the shallots until soft. Stir in the seasonings.
2. Cut the ends off the asparagus where the green stalk changes color and becomes tough. Cook the asparagus spears until just tender. Cut off the tops to measure 1" long and reserve for later.
3. Purée the stems in a food processor with the shallot mixture and the boiled potato.
4. Fill the artichoke bottoms, creating a mound. Top each with an asparagus top and place 2 strips of pimento criss-cross across the top for color. Brush lightly with olive oil, place on a greased cookie sheet and reheat at 300° for 5 minutes only.

Braised Endive

Serves 4 people

4 endives, cut into halves lengthwise
½ cup soy sauce
½ cup concentrated beef broth bouillon

1. Heat beef broth and soy sauce in a large skillet. Put endive in and simmer, uncovered, over a medium fire until lightly browned and soft.
2. Turn pieces of endive over carefully and brown on the other side.

NOTE: *This is an absoutely fabulous vegetable, and well worth the high price.*

Glazed Carrots

1 pound carrots, peeled and sliced into thick strips about 2" long
1 cup water or less, just to cover the bottom of the pot
4 tablespoons butter or margarine
3 tablespoons packed light brown sugar
Juice of 1 lemon
Juice of ½ orange

1. Cook carrots in water until just tender, covered. Drain.
2. Melt butter and add the brown sugar, lemon and orange and stir until dissolved. Stir in carrots and allow to get very hot before serving.

Stuffed Zucchini Boats

Serves 2 people as a vegetarian dinner or 4 people as a vegetable

2 large zucchini
¼ pound sliced fresh mushrooms
2 green onions (scallions)
Centers of zucchini, which have been cut out and chopped
1 tablespoon butter or margarine
1 small tomato, skinned and chopped
1 small yellow or red pepper, chopped
½ teaspoon ground oregano
½ teaspoon garlic powder or 1 clove fresh garlic
½ teaspoon chervil
1 tablespoon tomato paste
Salt and pepper to taste

1. Wash and slice zucchini into halves. Cut out centers to look like a "boat." Put "boats" into a skillet with just enough water to cover the bottom and steam, covered, until done but still firm. Put on paper toweling to dry.
2. Sauté vegetables and seasonings in butter until all liquid has been absorbed. Add tomato paste.
3. Spoon the mixture into the zucchini halves. Sprinkle lightly with Parmesan cheese. Set on a cookie sheet and broil until brown.

French Mushroom Delight

Serves 6–8 people for brunch or as a first course

20 Pâte-à-Chou (cream puffs), hors d'oeuvre size
1½ ounces butter
1 medium onion
6 ounces small mushrooms
1 tablespoon flour
½ cup chicken broth or white wine
1 teaspoon minced parsley
1 tablespoon finely-grated Parmesan cheese
1 tablespoon toasted breadcrumbs
6 strips bacon, cut into 4 squares and baked crisp in 300° oven

1. Melt half the butter and add the onion, finely chopped. Cook slowly until soft, but not colored.
2. Slice the mushrooms thin and sauté briskly for a minute or two.
3. Take the pan off the fire and add the remaining butter. When melted, blend in the flour and the stock. Stir until boiling. Season to taste with salt and pepper. Simmer for 5 minutes. Stir in parsley.
4. Butter a shallow casserole dish. Pour the mixture into the center and dust with grated cheese and crumbs mixed together. Put under the broiler until brown.
5. Place the cream puffs around the outside edge of the dish. Put a curl of bacon on top of each and bake at 300° for 5 minutes.

Spinach Casserole with Escargot

Serves 8 people

2 packages frozen spinach or 2 cups cooked fresh spinach
12 medium mushroom caps
⅛ teaspoon nutmeg
1 teaspoon finely-chopped parsley
1 clove crushed garlic
1 tablespoon dry vermouth
4 tablespoons butter or margarine
12 oysters or 12 large escargots (in can)
Salt and pepper
4 tablespoons butter or margarine
2 tablespoons flour
1 cup light cream or milk

1. Cook spinach until just done. Do not overcook. If fresh, chop well. Squeeze out all the water and set aside.
2. Melt 4 tablespoons butter. Add nutmeg, garlic, parsley, and vermouth. Stir. Allow to bubble for a few minutes. Add drained oysters or escargots. Stir well and allow to sit while fixing spinach.
3. Melt 4 tablespoons butter. Stir in flour and cream, and continue stirring until thick. Stir in cooked spinach and taste for salt and pepper. Spoon into a well-greased casserole dish.
4. Remove the stems from the mushrooms and reserve for another use. They may be chopped and added to the spinach, if you like. Melt a little butter and dip the mushroom caps into it. Place each cap attractively and evenly in rows across the top of the spinach. Fill each cap with 1 oyster or escargot. Just before placing on the buffet table heat the casserole in a 350° oven for no longer than 10 minutes.

Spinach and Oysters IFTT

Serves 4 people

16 whole fresh oysters
2 cups chopped spinach
4 tablespoons butter
4 tablespoons flour
1½ cups warm milk
½ cup liquid from the poached oysters
¾ cup grated Swiss cheese (food processor)
1½ teaspoon salt
1 teaspoon chopped tarragon
1 teaspoon finely-chopped parsley
2 tablespoons grated Swiss cheese

1. Poach the oysters in their own liquor for 30 seconds only and set aside.
2. Make a Mornay sauce by melting the butter in a saucepan, adding the flour, stirring constantly, and then adding the warm milk slowly while stirring until thick and smooth. Add the liquid from the oysters, and ¾ cup of the cheese.
3. Cook the spinach in a small amount of water and drain. Toss with the salt, tarragon, and parsley. Taste for salt and pepper to please your palate.
4. Mix half of the Mornay sauce into the spinach and put the mixture in an oven-proof dish or individual casseroles. Top with the oysters. Pour the rest of the Mornay sauce over the top and sprinkle the 2 tablespoons grated cheese lightly around.
5. Place under the broiler until brown and bubbly.

NOTE: May be made in the morning, reheated in the casserole at 300° for 10 minutes and then broiled.

Spinach Pies

Greek style

1 pound chopped raw spinach or 2 packages frozen
3 eggs
½ pound crumbled Feta or Ricotta cheese
1 teaspoon fresh dill weed
2 tablespoons fresh chopped mint leaves
½ cup chopped chives or scallion greens
1 teaspoon salt
½ teaspoon pepper
2 tablespoons melted butter
1 pound phyllo dough

1. Beat the eggs and stir in the cheese, the dill, mint, scallion greens, salt and pepper. Combine with the spinach and pour in the melted butter.
2. Cut phyllo dough into strips 4½" wide. Use two sheets for each pie. Brush with melted butter. Place a tablespoon of the spinach filling onto the sheet and follow the directions on page 57 to fold. Bake at 375° for about 20 minutes, or until crisp and brown.

Squash Soufflé

Serves 8 people

4 acorn squash, baked for 1½ hours, or until very done
4 egg whites, beaten thick with ½ teaspoon cream of tartar
1 cup crushed canned pineapple (in its own juice), drained
2 tablespoons cinnamon
6 tablespoons white sugar
¼ teaspoon salt
Melted butter and cornflake crumbs, tossed to create a thick
    topping

1. Mash squash.
2. Combine squash, pineapple, cinnamon, sugar, and salt.
3. Beat egg whites with cream of tartar and fold into squash. Spoon into a casserole.
4. Combine cornflake crumbs with melted butter to a flaky mixture and spoon lavishly over the top. Bake at 325° for 15–20 minutes.

Eggplant Parmesan

1 medium eggplant
6 peeled and chopped tomatoes
1 finely-chopped small onion
2 tablespoons olive oil
3 tablespoons tomato paste
½ teaspoon oregano
Pinch of salt and pepper
¾ cup freshly-grated Parmesan cheese
1½ teaspoon chopped fresh parsley
¼ cup plain toasted breadcrumbs
Shredded Mozzarella cheese

1. Peel and slice the eggplant into ½" slices. Put a tablespoon of salt into a bowl of ice water and soak the slices for 30 minutes. Drain off water. Pat the slices dry with paper toweling.
2. Peel and chop the tomatoes and sauté with the onion in the oil. Stir in the tomato paste and oregano, salt and pepper. Set aside.
3. Fry the eggplant slices in another pan in a small amount of olive oil. Drain on absorbent paper. (Eggplant absorbs oil.)
4. Spread a thin layer of the tomato mixture on the bottom of an 8" glass baking dish. Put a layer of eggplant, a layer of tomato mixture, then a layer of eggplant.
5. Top with combined Parmesan, parsley, and breadcrumbs and sprinkle a bit of shredded Mozzarella over all.
6. Bake uncovered at 350° until brown and bubbly (about 30 minutes).

Stuffed Mushrooms

Serves 12 people

12 huge mushrooms—white and very fresh
¼ pound mild sweet Italian sausage, cooked and crumbled
2 tablespoons breadcrumbs (Buy Italian preseasoned, but don't tell
    anyone)
1 egg, beaten
¼ pound butter, melted
1 ounce dry white wine
½ cup finely-crumbled Mozzarella cheese

1. Clean mushrooms either by peeling off outer layer or rinsing
   quickly under cool water and drying on paper toweling.
2. Remove stems and reserve for another use. (They give excellent flavor to all gravies.)
3. Combine the cooked sausage, breadcrumbs, and egg and stuff
   the caps. Place into a shallow baking dish with melted butter
   and wine and bake for 15 minutes at 350°.
4. Sprinkle cheese on top and broil until brown and bubbly. Serve
   as a vegetable with chicken or as a first course on the same
   plate as Baked Clams or Clams Casino.

Swiss Cabbage with Apples

Serves 6 people

1 large red cabbage
1 large onion, diced fine by hand or in a food processor
4 tablespoons unsalted butter
2 apples, unpeeled and grated or diced fine in a food processor
¾ cup red Port wine
1¼ cup (1 10-ounce can) beef broth bouillon
1 tablespoon freshly-chopped dill weed
1 teaspoon caraway seed
1 tablespoon white sugar
2 tablespoons wine vinegar (white or red)

1. Cut the cabbage in half. Remove the white hard core at the bottom and cut the leaves into fine long strips.
2. Dice the onion fine and sauté it in the butter until just soft.
3. Add the cabbage, a little at a time, stirring well so it will be perfectly mixed with the onions. Allow to cook very slowly until soft (about 10 minutes).
4. Stir in the wine and the bouillon and add the dill, caraway, sugar, and the grated apples. Cover the pan and simmer for at least 1½ to 2 hours. Stir in the vinegar and simmer another 10 minutes. Serve with pork, ham, or game.

Artichokes Stuffed with Shrimp

Serves 6 people

6 large artichokes
1 pound tiny shrimp, fresh or frozen: peeled, cooked, and cleaned
½ pound butter
2 shallots, chopped fine (or, 1 small onion)
½ green pepper, chopped fine
2 cloves garlic, crushed
¼ cup dry white vermouth
2 teaspoons chopped dill
2 teaspoons chopped parsley
1 teaspoon powdered thyme
1 cup breadcrumbs

1. Cut stems and tops from artichokes ⅓ from the tops with a sharp serrated knife. Cut thorns neatly off with a sharp scissors. (This takes a few minutes but the result is a flower instead of a cactus!) Bring artichokes to a boil in enough water to cover in a large pot. Boil hard, covered, until tender. Do not overcook. Artichokes are done when a leaf can be pulled out easily. If overdone, they will fall apart. Small ones take 15–20 minutes. Large ones take about 30 minutes.
2. Remove artichokes from pot with tongs and turn upside down to drain. When still warm, remove the centers and prickly fibers with a small spoon being careful not to cut into any of the bottoms. Cool.
3. Cook shallots, pepper, garlic, vermouth, dill, parsley, and thyme for 10 minutes together over a medium fire. Stir in the breadcrumbs and the cooked shrimp.
4. Loosely fill centers of artichokes, piling mixture high. Place artichokes on a cookie sheet and put in a 400° oven for 3 minutes. Top each with a cooked shrimp and serve with a side dish of melted butter for dipping leaves.

NOTE: Steps #1–#3 may be made in the morning.

Pita Cottontails

Pitas for 4 people

4 pita pockets
2 carrots
1 zucchini
½ pound mushrooms
Choice of broccoli, cauliflower, red pepper, green pepper, or all to
    equal 1 cup when chopped
¼ teaspoon powdered ginger
⅛ teaspoon powdered garlic
⅛ teaspoon black pepper
¼ cup light soy sauce
2 cups (16 ounces) sour cream
Bean or alfalfa sprouts for garnish (optional)

1. Chop the vegetables approximately ¼" in size and put in a steamer or a tiny amount of water. Cover tightly and cook until barely tender and still crunchy. Drain and set aside.
2. Combine sour cream with seasonings and soy sauce.
3. Just before filling pita pockets, heat the sour cream mixture and toss in vegetables. Stuff pockets. Leave pitas whole or cut in halves and put sprouts in the openings. Serve with pickles, olives, tomatoes, and chips.

NOTE: If you don't have facilities to heat the filling, the Pita Cottontails are just as good cold.

This is a marvelous meal for football Sundays or a business lunch in the office. Steam and chop your vegetables in advance. Buy the Pita pockets and the rest of the ingredients and put together at the last minute.

VARIATION: Diced chicken, ham, bacon, or shrimp may be added. Just eliminate some of the vegetables.

Zucchini Bundles

Zucchini
Chive strands, or green strands from spring onions
Butter
Salt

1. Boil strands until just soft so they will not break when tied around the zucchini.
2. Do not peel the zucchini. Cut it into julienne very thin strips all the same length. Tie into little bundles with the chive strands.
3. Steam the zucchini in a basket or very little water until just done. Brush lightly with melted butter and sprinkle a little salt over before serving.

NOTE: Carrots, celery, or turnips may also be served in this way.

Potatoes, Dumplings, Pasta, Pizza, and Rice

The Potato

The potato plant grows wild in the elevated regions throughout South America. It was supposedly brought back to Spain and Portugal by the Spanish sailors before 1560. In 1563, Sir John Hawkins is said to have introduced the potato into England, and Sir Francis Drake supposedly obtained potatoes in the West Indies and returned to Ireland with them in 1586. Potatoes became one of the most popular foods on the ships, because they stored for long periods of time, and because it was found that the potato was a partial preventative of scurvy. It is a misconception that Sir Walter Raleigh found the Indians of Virginia growing potatoes, and that he returned to England and Ireland with them. Potatoes did not come from the American Indians. Although little is known about their introduction to North America, legend has it that the English brought them to Bermuda in 1613, and from there they were brought to the colonists of Virginia and Carolina. The most authentic report shows that potatoes were first grown at Londonderry, New Hampshire, in 1719, from stock brought in by Irish immigrants. For that reason the white potato was, and still is, called the Irish potato in many places. The white potato, by the way, is not related to the sweet potato or yam.

The last people to accept the potato in western Europe were the French. The potato supposedly went from Spain to Italy, where it became exceedingly popular in the northern region. The French, however, refused to accept this new vegetable, and, in 1771, the potato was still said to be unfit for human consumption. It was, in fact, labeled dangerous, because of its "weakening properties." During this same year a man by the name of Parmentier wrote a thesis, listing the potato among the vegetables, which could be eaten in times of food shortage along with horse-chestnuts, acorns, and gladioli. In 1787, during just such a time, he bought 50 acres of poor farm land and grew potatoes. However, only the white and purple flower became popular as an inedible ornament on the dinner plate of the upper class. It wasn't until the 19th century that the potato became one of the staple foods in France.

The potato contains thiamin, riboflavin, niacin, ascorbic acid, vitamin A, calcium, iron, magnesium, phosphorus, potassium, and sodium. The best method of cooking to preserve the maximum of its mineral elements and the maximum taste is to bake it in the oven. The taste is most defined this way, so salt needn't be added if the diet is restricted. To avoid loss of mineral salts and potassium salts, do not boil it in too much water when boiled. This loss is further decreased when cooked in fat or oil instead of water.

Glazed Sweet Potatoes with Triple Sec

4 large sweet potatoes
¼ cup fresh orange juice
1 tablespoon Triple Sec or Grand Marnier
¼ teaspoon cinnamon
1 cup dark brown sugar
½ cup butter

1. Boil the potatoes with their skins on until done.
2. Cool slightly and peel. Slice on the round approximately 1" thick.
3. Put into a baking dish.
4. Combine orange juice, Triple Sec, sugar, cinnamon, and butter in a saucepan and bring to a boil, stirring constantly. Pour over potatoes and bake at 350° for about 10 minutes. Baste and serve.

NOTE: *Triple Sec is generally less expensive than Grand Marnier and serves the same taste sensation.*

Gnocchi

6 large potatoes
3 egg yolks
1 teaspoon salt
2 cups flour

1. Boil potatoes until very soft. Remove skins. Mash with the egg yolks and salt in a large bowl or electric mixer fit with a bread hook. Add the flour, one cup at a time, and knead the mixture by hand or with the bread hook until the consistency of bread dough (smooth but not sticky). Refrigerate until very cold.
2. Cut the dough into 4 equal parts and roll each part with the hands into long pieces about 1" around. Slice into 1" pieces. Roll each piece with the palms of the hands until it resembles a small cone at each end with a fat middle.
3. Fill a soup pot with salted water and cook the gnocchi as you would pasta until the gnocchi are done—about 10 minutes— taste for doneness. They should be soft but chewy.
4. Remove with a slotted spoon and serve with butter, tomato or meat sauce, cheese or cream sauce.

NOTE: I don't know whether to classify gnocchi as a pasta or a dumpling, because it can be eaten in such a variety of ways.

If you bake the potatoes instead of boiling them, your family can feast on the potato skins as well. Serve them buttered, or with garlic, or filled with tomato sauce and mozzarella and browned under the broiler.

Potato Pancakes

Food processor method

1 pound potatoes
1 small onion
1 beaten egg
1 tablespoon flour
½ teaspoon baking powder
½ teaspoon salt
Pinch of white pepper

1. Put the onion and potato in the food processor and pulvarize.
2. Add the egg and turn the processor on/off once quickly.
3. Combine flour, baking powder, salt and pepper, and add to the processor. Turn on/off quickly 2 times until blended.
4. Drop by spoonsful into a skillet in ½″ vegetable oil or peanut oil on a high fire. Fry on both sides until brown. Drain on paper toweling. Keep warm in a 200° oven on a heatproof platter while cooking the rest.

Macaroni with Gorgonzola

Serves 4 people

4 cups cooked macaroni (large)
4 cooked artichoke bottoms (fresh or canned) cut into quarters
4 eggs
½ cup crumbled Gorgonzola or Blue cheese
¼ cup olive oil

1. Soak the artichoke bottoms in the oil for 15 minutes.
2. Cook the macaroni and drain off the water.
3. Put into a casserole and toss with the olive oil.
4. Beat the eggs well and stir in the artichoke hearts and the crumbled cheese.
5. Toss the cheese mixture into the macaroni.
6. Bake in a 400° oven for 8–10 minutes. Serve immediately.

NOTE: *The better quality the cheese the better the sauce!*

Matzo Balls

4 tablespoons very cold chicken fat
2 eggs
½ cup sifted matzo meal
½ teaspoon salt
⅛ teaspoon white pepper
⅛ teaspoon nutmeg (or less)
1 full teaspoon ice water

1. Combine chicken fat and eggs in a bowl and beat by hand or with an electric beater until just frothy.
2. Presift the matzo meal with the salt and pepper and nutmeg and add to eggs. Beat well and add the ice water. Beat well again. Cover and refrigerate for several hours or overnight.
3. Rinse your hands in cold water and form balls the size of large walnuts. Drop into boiling soup and boil gently, partially covered, (leave just enough air space for steam to escape), for 45 minutes or until done. Leave in the soup to cool and refrigerate.

NOTE: *Soup evaporates when it boils. To avoid losing my good soup I sometimes boil the matzo balls in a weak solution of canned chicken broth.*

This recipe may be doubled or tripled for a crowd. Cut back on the white pepper when you double.

Matzo Balls are a unique dumpling; easy to make in advance. They can be served with soup or on the plate with chicken in place of a potato. They are one of my favorite dumplings served with Bassano Roast.

Allen's "Drop Dead" Meatless Pasta Sauce

Serves 4 people

3 cloves crushed garlic
2 tablespoons chopped fresh parsley
2 tablespoons Italian olive oil
1 large Bermuda onion, chopped fine
½ cup pitted black Greek or black spiced olives, sliced in halves
½ cup green Pimento olives, sliced in halves
32 ounces stewed tomatoes (canned)
¼ cup pimento strips
1 small red pepper, chopped fine
1 small green pepper, chopped fine
8–10 bottled or fresh Tuscan peppers
1 or 2 chopped fresh basil leaves
1 jar capers
1 tin anchovies (rolled with capers)

1. Sauté garlic, onion, and parsley until soft. Add the rest of the ingredients except the anchovies. Simmer for 1 hour on a very slow fire.
2. Serve over any pasta.

NOTE: This recipe originates from Allen Marcus, an interior designer extraordinaire and a super cook! This pasta with a good salad is all one needs for sheer happiness.

Vongole CA 7 with Linguine

Dinner for 2 people

2 dozen medium-sized clams, or 4 dozen tiny clams (well-washed)
2 large cloves minced garlic
1 minced shallot
¼ cup olive oil (Italian Extra Virgin only)
1 cup rich beef broth, or 1 10-ounce can Campbell's Bouillon
4 tablespoons freshly-chopped parsley
Freshly-ground pepper to taste
Linguine pasta (fresh is best, although there are some wonderful
   pastas freshly frozen, which can be found in specialty gourmet
   stores)

1. Sauté garlic and shallot in the olive oil for 5 minutes over a medium fire. Add the beef broth and the clams. Cover and bring to a boil. Cook just until the clams pop open.
2. At the same time the clams are cooking, cook the linguine in another pot with a little salt until done but *very* firm. Drain off water.
3. Pour the clams and liquid over the linguine. Add the parsley and grind as much pepper as pleases you over. Toss very well. Serve immediately.

NOTE: The original recipe comes from my favorite restaurant in Italy: CA 7, in Bassano del Grappa, a small town set into the mountains north of Venice. The shallot was not in the recipe, but I think it adds flavor. If you cannot find shallots, chop up green spring onions. The clams in Bassano are no larger than your thumbnail, and they are piled in an enormous mound over the linguine. It takes a good 30 minutes to remove them from their shells and neccessitates a shower afterwards! This is one of the best dishes I have ever eaten.

Spinach Canneloni

Serves 6 people

3 cups cooked, coarsely-chopped fresh spinach
4 tablespoons minced onion
1 large minced fresh basil leaf or ½ teaspoon dried basil
⅛ teaspoon nutmeg
2 tablespoons minced fresh parsley
8 tablespoons (¼ pound) butter
½ cup finely-chopped baked ham
1¼ cups Ricotta cheese
½ cup freshly-grated Parmesan cheese
½ cup freshly-grated Swiss cheese
2 egg yolks

1. Make or buy lasagne pasta. Cut into pieces approximately 4" x 8" and boil in salted water for 5 minutes only.
2. Cook the spinach and drain well, squeezing out excess water.
3. Melt butter and sauté onion until light in color. Add basil, nutmeg, parsley, and ham. Remove from fire.
4. Stir in spinach.
5. Stir in Ricotta cheese and egg yolks.
6. Stir in other cheeses.
7. Put a good amount onto the end of a strip of pasta and roll up. Place flap side down in buttered individual baking dishes (oval, if you have them). Cover with plastic wrap until later.
8. Cover with a layer of Béchamel Sauce, sprinkle with Parmesan cheese, and bake at 400° until very hot and browned on top.

Pasta Verde with Cheese and Ham

Serves 8 people as a first course or 4 people for dinner

4 cups, in total, of crumbled Swiss, Gruyère, and Parmesan
  cheeses, which have been put into the food processor in equal
  parts
1 pound diced baked ham (in food processor)
6 tablespoons butter
6 tablespoons flour
4 cups milk
¼ teaspoon nutmeg
2 eggs, beaten

1. Make or buy lasagne pasta. Cut pasta into squares and cook for
   only 3-4 minutes in salted, boiling water. Cut again to the size
   of individual oval ramekins (small for the first course; larger for
   dinner). Count 4 squares for each ramekin.
2. Melt butter and stir in flour in a pot.
3. Pour milk slowly into butter and flour, stirring until smooth
   and thick.
4. Add nutmeg and crumbled cheeses and stir until cheese has
   melted.
5. Remove from heat and stir a bit of the hot mixture into the
   beaten egg. Then stir all of the egg into the hot mixture.
6. Return to heat and cook over medium-low heat, stirring constantly, until very thick.
7. Cool slightly and spoon, in a thin layer, onto the first layer of
   pasta, which has been placed in the buttered ramekins.
8. Sprinkle the ham over the sauce.
9. Add a layer of pasta and spoon more sauce over. Do not put
   ham on this layer.
10. Add another layer of pasta, spoon sauce over it, sprinkle with
    ham.
11. Repeat Step #10. There will be four layers in all.
12. Cover the entire top with a Thin Béchamel Sauce (page 160).
13. Sprinkle grated Parmesan cheese over the tops and bake at 250°
    for 10 minutes. Put the oven on broil and broil until browned.
    Serve at once.

Thin Béchamel Sauce

2 tablespoons butter
1 tablespoon flour
2 cups whole milk
1 bay leaf
⅛ teaspoon black pepper

1. Melt the butter in a saucepan. Stir in the flour, milk, bay leaf, and pepper, and simmer over a very low fire for ten minutes. Remove bay leaf and pour over pasta.

Northern Italian Style Rice and Dried Mushrooms

1½ cups white rice
1 cup dried mushrooms
¼ pound butter plus ¼ cup Italian olive oil
1 clove crushed garlic
1 medium onion, minced, or 2 shallots, chopped fine
2 cups rich chicken broth (homemade is best)
2 cups water (or more)
Salt and pepper to taste

1. Soak the mushrooms in boiling hot water until soft and spongy. Drain and wash. Chop.
2. Sauté the garlic, onion, and mushrooms for a few minutes in two tablespoons butter and the olive oil. Add the chicken broth and the rice and cook over a very low fire, uncovered, for 45 minutes, stirring every once in a while and adding water as needed for moisture. Stir once again. Add the remaining water, and cover. Reduce heat to simmer and allow to stand 30 minutes.
3. Stir in the remaining butter and salt and pepper to taste.

NOTE: For a marvelous taste sensation substitute champagne for the water.

Pizza

Makes 1 large (12") round pizza

2 cups unsifted bread flour
½ teaspoon salt
1 teaspoon dry, active powdered yeast
½ teaspoon white sugar
¾ cup warm water
2 cups shredded Mozzarella cheese
1 15-ounce bottle commercial marinara sauce
Powdered oregano, minced garlic, pepperoni, salami, green
    pepper, onions, mushrooms, capers, anchovies, hamburger
    meat, olives, artichoke hearts, or even seafood for a change.

1. Put the flour and salt into a bowl.
2. Combine the oil, yeast, sugar, and water in a cup and stir until
   blended.
3. Pour the yeast mixture into the flour and knead until smooth
   and elastic. ("To Knead" simply means punch it down, squeeze
   it together, pull it apart, and push it together until it looks
   smooth. It may take anywhere from 1–5 minutes, depending
   on the strength in your hands.) Shape into a round ball. Punch
   a hole in the center. Put it into the bowl. Cover the bowl with a
   damp towel. Allow to rise for 1 hour.
4. Set the dough onto the pizza pan and pull it evenly all the way
   to the edges. Pat it down.
5. Spoon the sauce over the top and sprinkle with oregano,
   garlic, or anything else, such as basil, onion powder, etc.
   Cover lavishly with your choice and top with the cheese.
6. Bake in a preheated 375° oven for 30–35 minutes, or until the
   crust is brown.

NOTE: *The southern Italians brush the top with olive oil before cooking for a
glossy pizza and they put the cheese under the vegetables. The pizza may be
prepared in the morning and refrigerated covered, until ready to cook. Allow to
come to room temperature before cooking (about 15 minutes).*

Rice Pilaf

Serves 6 people

2 cups rice
6 ounces curly vermicelli or angel hair pasta
1 teaspoon pepper
½ cup butter
4 cups rich chicken broth (3 10-ounce cans Campbell's
Concentrated Chicken Broth)
2 cups water

1. Melt butter in a deep skillet or medium-sized pot.
2. Break up the pasta into uneven pieces and put it with the rice into the bubbling butter. Cook over a medium-high fire, turning constantly with a wooden spoon, until very brown, but not burned.
3. Add pepper and chicken broth and water. Bring to a boil. Stir once. Cover. Reduce heat to simmer, and cook slowly until done (about 20 minutes). If pilaf looks dry, add another can of chicken broth. It should be served moist.

Note: This is my favorite recipe for family and company. It is a perfect accompaniment to chicken, fish, shrimp, pork, or even scrambled eggs.

Wild Rice Ring

Serves 4 people

1 6-ounce box wild rice
8 tablespoons butter or margarine (¼ pound)
1 finely-chopped large onion
2 finely-chopped pieces of celery
8–10 large mushrooms cut into small cubes
¾ cup water
1¼ cups concentrated chicken broth
1 teaspoon salt
1 teaspoon black pepper
1-quart ring mold

1. Place wild rice in a large pot and pour boiling water over to cover. Let stand until water is cool; about ½ hour. Drain and set aside.
2. Sauté the onions and celery in the butter until soft and golden in color.
3. Add the mushrooms, chicken broth and water, and allow to come to a boil.
4. Add rice, salt, and pepper, and stir. Turn to low when mixture reaches a good boil. Cook, covered, for 1 hour. Turn off heat and leave, untouched, until ready to serve. Fluff with 2 forks and serve, or fill an oiled ring mold. This part may be done in the morning.
5. Set mold into a pan of water and bake at 350°, covered with foil, for 30–40 minutes. Turn upside down onto a platter and allow to sit for a few minutes. Pull the mold slowly straight up. Fill the center with sautéed mushrooms.

A Different Rice

8 cups water
½ cup dried mushrooms
3 large leeks
1 teaspoon curry powder
1 large green pepper
3 large plum tomatoes
3 cups white rice

1. Soak the mushrooms in very hot water for 15 minutes. Chop them coarsely.
2. Cut off the white part of the leeks and chop them coarsely.
3. Skin the tomatoes and chop. Chop the green pepper.
4. Boil the water with the mushrooms, leeks, curry powder, green pepper and tomatoes for 30 minutes. Stir in 3 cups white rice and cook over a medium fire until all the liquid is absorbed.

Salads

Cold Carrot Relish

2 pounds carrots, cut into strips and cooked until ALMOST done
   (about 4–5 minutes)
1 green pepper, cut into strips
2 onions, sweet, sliced on the round very thin
1 10-ounce can tomato soup (condensed Campbell's)
1 cup granulated sugar
¾ cup vinegar
½ cup oil
1 tablespoon brown mustard
1 tablespoon Worcestershire sauce
Minced fresh parsley

1. Cook carrots and allow to cool.
2. Combine carrots with the rest of the ingredients and marinate overnight in a covered dish. Sprinkle with parsley. Serve very cold.

NOTE: This recipe originated from Gretchen Bailey.

Mango, Pear, or Peach Chutney

6 cups mango, pear, or peach, peeled and diced into cubes (about
   8 mangoes or 14 peaches or pears)
2 large onions, chopped into small pieces by hand
2 green peppers, chopped into small pieces by hand
4 ounces finely-sliced dried, sweetened ginger (Paradise or
   Dromedary)
6 ounces bottled, preserved stem candied ginger, chopped
   (Raffetto)
1 tablespoon ground ginger, or a 3" piece green ginger root, peeled
3 tablespoons minced or crushed garlic
2 limes, juice and zest
1 generous tablespoon powdered cinnamon
1 teaspoon powdered cloves
1 tablespoon ground allspice
1 teaspoon salt
4 cups golden raisins
4 cups dark brown sugar
20 ounces red wine vinegar

1. Chop onions and green peppers by hand. Do not use food
   processor. Consistency should be chunky and not uniform.
2. Put all ingredients into a soup pot and bring to a boil. Cook
   uncovered, stirring occasionally, over a medium fire for 1 hour.
   Taste. If too tart, add more brown sugar to taste. Cook another
   half hour. Cool completely. Remove ginger root and spoon into
   airtight jars. Refrigerate. Serve with fish, lamb, duck, pork, or
   chicken. It's also marvelous over ice cream.

NOTE: Chutney improves as the flavors marry. These ingredients will bring
about a really good relationship after several weeks. It should last almost a year.
("Like many marriages of today.")

Grandma Elsa's Raw Cranberry Mold

An old-fashioned favorite for Thanksgiving, Christmas, or Easter

1 pound raw cranberries
2 oranges, quartered, skins on
1 lemon, skin on
2 cups sugar
9 ounces raspberry Jello (3 3-ounce packages)
2 cups boiling water
2 cups cold water
2 cups chopped walnuts

1. Put the cranberries, oranges and lemon through a grinder. (Or, in the food processor fitted with the steel blade. Keep the mixture rather coarse.)
2. Add the sugar to the cranberry mixture and allow to dissolve for 15 minutes.
3. Make the Jello with the hot water and cold water. Stir the nuts and cranberry mixture into it and pour into a 2½-quart oiled ring mold.
4. Allow to mold overnight. Turn out onto a platter and fill the center of the mold with kumquats and decorate with mint leaves.

NOTE: Use a vegetable liquid oil to oil the mold, taking any excess oil away by rubbing with a paper towel. When you oil a mold well there is no need to pour water over it to unmold. Simply take a sharp knife around the edge, and turn onto the platter. The mold will slide out by itself.

Watercress and Endive Salad

Serves 4 people

1 unpeeled cucumber sliced thin
4 bunches watercress
2 endives, cut into long strips
1 tablespoon each: parsley, chervil, chives, tarragon
¼ teaspoon each: salt and pepper
1 teaspoon yellow mustard
4 thickly sliced large white mushrooms
1 cup Italian olive oil
½ cup tarragon vinegar
1 tablespoon white sugar
1 hard boiled egg, white and yolk riced separately
4 cherry tomatoes

1. Combine parsley, chervil, chives, tarragon, salt and pepper with the oil and allow to sit for 1 hour. Add vinegar and sugar.
2. Slice cucumbers thin and sprinkle well with salt. Let them stand for 3 hours in a strainer or colander. Remove to a bowl. Pour ⅓ of the dressing over to marinate for another 2 hours.
3. Pour ⅓ of the dressing over the watercress and toss well just before serving.
4. Pour ⅓ of the dressing over the endive and toss well just before serving.
5. Place cucumbers, watercress, and endive individually onto the salad plates. Slice the mushrooms across the center. Sprinkle the two colors of riced egg artistically around. Top each with a cherry tomato.

NOTE: This is sooo *pretty and* sooo *good!*

Shrimp Mold and Gazpacho Aspic

Serves 16–20 people

2 pounds large shrimp, cooked, cleaned, and cut into halves
lengthwise
2 onions
Handful of parsley
2 cloves garlic, crushed
2 green peppers
6 pieces celery
3 tomatoes, skinned (Italian plum style, if available)
23 ounces tomato juice
16 ounces bloody mary mix (in can or bottle)
8 tablespoons unflavored gelatin
1 cucumber, peeled and coarsely chopped
2 raw zucchini, peeled and coarsely chopped
2 8-ounce cans water chestnuts, sliced
Garnish: Cucumbers in center of mold, which have been sliced
thin and marinated overnight in vinegar, sugar, and salt to taste

1. Put the onion, celery, parsley, garlic, and peppers into the food
   processor and, using the steel blade, chop fine. Put into a soup
   pot. Chop the tomatoes by hand and add to the pot.
2. Add the tomato juice and the bloody mary mix. Bring to a boil
   and boil gently for 5 minutes.
3. Dissolve gelatin in ½ cup (or more) warm water and stir a bit of
   the tomato mixture into it before pouring it into the pot. Stir
   well.
4. Stir in the cucumber, zucchini, and water chestnuts. Add the
   shrimp. Pour into a well-greased large ring mold and refrigerate overnight or until very cold and firm. Unmold and fill with
   the cucumbers, which have been well-drained.

Caesar Salad

Large salad for 2 people

1 head Romaine lettuce
¼ teaspoon dry mustard, or 1 teaspoon Dijon mustard
2 cloves crushed garlic
6 anchovy fillets
½ teaspoon salt
¼ teaspoon black pepper
¼ teaspoon Worcestershire sauce
Juice from 2 medium-sized lemons
1 cup good Italian olive oil
1 tablespoon red wine vinegar
½ cup freshly-grated Parmesan cheese
2 eggs, coddled
Homemade croutons
Whole peppercorns to grind over top
Parmesan cheese for the top

1. Separate the lettuce leaves, wash well under cold water, and roll up into a dish towel. Refrigerate.
2. Combine the mustard, garlic, two of the anchovy fillets, salt, pepper, worcestershire sauce, lemon juice, olive oil and vinegar in a blender and blend on low speed. Pour into a small bowl or cup.
3. Coddle the egg by boiling it for 10 seconds only. Remove from the water but do not break open.
4. Make croutons by simmering ¼ pound butter with 1 garlic clove, ⅛ teaspoon oregano, ⅛ teaspoon thyme, and a pinch of nutmeg for 5 minutes. Brush heavily onto sliced French bread (sliced lengthwise). Sprinkle with a bit of grated Parmesan cheese, and bake at 200° for ½ hour. Remove from oven, cut into small squares while still hot and return to the oven, which has been turned off, for another ½ hour.
5. To serve: Take lettuce from the refrigerator and tear it into large pieces in a salad bowl. Toss with the dressing. Break the egg and toss it through the leaves until they are coated. Divide salad into two portions on 7" or 9" plates. Top each with 2 anchovies and the croutons and grate pepper and extra cheese over individually.

Tomato Aspic

3 cups tomato juice
2 tablespoons mixed whole pickling spice
3 tablespoons gelatin, dissolved in ½ cup lukewarm water
Juice from 1 lemon
8 tablespoons cottage cheese mixed with 2 tablespoons chopped
    chives

1. Bring tomato juice and pickling spice to a boil and simmer for ten minutes. Cool and strain.
2. Soften gelatin and stir into the hot tomato mixture. Add lemon juice and pour into an oiled (vegetable oil) ring mold and chill until "spongy."
3. Drop the cottage cheese, which has been mixed with the chives, into the mold at equal distances apart, creating a design of red and white. Allow to become solid (overnight best). Unmold and fill the center with cucumbers freshly mixed with sour cream and chives.

Sour Cream Cole Slaw

Serves 6 people

1 head finely shredded cabbage
Salt to taste
1 cup sour cream
2 tablespoons sugar
1 teaspoon salt
1 teaspoon dry mustard
4 tablespoons lemon juice
1 tablespoon sweet pickle relish (or more)
Freshly grated black pepper

1. Mix dry ingredients. Add cream and lemon juice. Toss with cabbage.
2. Portion onto salad plates. Top each mound of slaw with a sprinkling of pickle relish. Grate fresh pepper over, if desired.

Dot's Family Favorite

4 3-ounce packages black cherry flavored Jello
3 cups boiling water
2 28-ounce cans pitted bing cherries
1 cup Port wine or Harvey's Bristol Cream
1 cup chopped walnuts (optional)

1. Bring 3 cups water to a boil, add Jello and stir until dissolved.
2. Drain cherries and add sufficient water to cherry juice to make 2 more cups. Combine juice with wine and add to the dissolved gelatin. Pour into an oiled 2 quart jello or bundt mold. Refrigerate until it reaches the consistency of soft jelly.
3. Fold in cherries (and nuts) and refrigerate until firm.
4. Unmold and serve.

NOTE: This was the "secret" recipe of a beautiful lady who brought it to our house each Thanksgiving.

Dessert Cakes

Apple Cake

Torte

2½ cups finely-chopped apples
1 teaspoon lemon juice
¼ cup dark brown sugar
¼ cup white sugar
¼ cup butter
1 teaspoon cinnamon
⅛ teaspoon nutmeg
1 teaspoon baking soda
1 teaspoon double-acting baking powder

1. Peel and chop the apples. Toss with the lemon juice.
2. Cream the butter and sugar until well blended with a hand electric mixer on high speed.
3. Beat in the egg on high speed until light and creamy.
4. Combine the flour, cinnamon, nutmeg, baking powder and baking soda and sift them into the wet ingredients. Mix well. Mixture will be very stiff.
5. Stir in the apples, and spoon into a 8" cake pan with a removable bottom.
6. Top with a mixture of:

   2 teaspoons flour
   2 teaspoons cinnamon
   ½ scant cup dark brown sugar
   1 cup coarsely-chopped pecans
   6 tablespoons softened butter

7. Slice half an apple and set it around the top attractively. Bake 35–40 minutes in a preheated 350° oven.

NOTE: Serve hot with vanilla ice cream.

Fudgie Brownies

Rich and Chocolaty! A Big Batch!

1 cup butter (½ pound) at room temperature
2 cups sugar
4 eggs
4 ounces unsweetened chocolate
4 teaspoons good Dutch cocoa
2 teaspoons vanilla extract
1¼ cups all purpose flour, sifted
1½ cups chopped pecans or walnuts (optional)

1. Melt chocolate over simmering water in a double boiler. Do not stir. When melted, remove from heat and cover to cool.
2. Cream butter and sugar on high speed of an electric mixer until white and fluffy. Scrape sides 2 times during creaming. Lower speed to medium.
3. Add eggs, one at a time, beating well after each addition. Scrape sides and bottom and beat another few seconds.
4. Add vanilla.
5. Measure flour and mix with cocoa. Add on lowest speed or by hand. Do not overbeat.
6. Fold in nuts.
7. Cut a piece of waxed paper to fit the bottom of a 13" x 9" x 2" pan and pour in the batter.
8. Bake in a preheated 350° oven 30 minutes. Toothpick will come out wet. Allow to cool and cut into squares.

NOTE: This recipe may be cut in half and cooked in a 8" x 8" pan.

Chocolate Hazelnut Torte Without Flour

10 large eggs at room temperature
1 cup sugar
¼ cup hazelnut liqueur (Frangelico)
6 ounce good sweet chocolate, dark or light
1½ cups finely-chopped or ground hazelnuts
1 large mixing bowl (not stainless steel)

1. Preheat oven to 350°.
2. Place the bowl over a pot of simmering water, and beat the eggs and sugar on high speed of a hand electric mixer until very light and thick (mousse-like). This should take approximately 10 minutes. Remove from the heat and continue beating for 5 more minutes.
3. Melt the chocolate and beat it in on a high speed.
4. Slowly beat in the Frangelico.
5. Fold in the nuts.
6. Pour into four 9″ buttered cake tins, which have been lined with wax paper, and bake for 25 minutes, or until a toothpick inserted comes out clean. Turn upside down onto wax paper and cool. Carefully remove wax paper, which will have stuck to the cake bottoms.
7. Fill with *Hazelnut liqueur filling:*

   2 pints heavy cream for whipping
   1 cup granulated sugar
   ½ cup hazelnut liqueur (Frangelico)

1. Beat the cream and sugar until almost thick. Slowly pour in the liqueur, beating until very thick. Fill the layers and cover the cake heavily. Pipe remaining cream through a piping tube to create rosettes on the sides and top.

Party-Sized Rich Chocolate Layer Cake

Serves 20–25 people

12 ounces semi-sweet chocolate, melted
1 cup unsalted butter, room temperature
2 cups dark brown sugar
4 whole eggs, room temperature
¼ cup coffee liqueur
1½ cups heavy cream
4 cups flour, sifted with 4 teaspoons baking powder and 3
    tablespoons unsweetened cocoa

1. Cream butter and sugar until very light and fluffy on highest speed of an electric mixer. Reduce speed to medium and add eggs, one at a time, until well-blended. Scrape the sides of the bowl.
2. Beat in the melted chocolate and liqueur. Reduce speed to low and beat in ⅓ of the cream; then ⅓ of the flour. Repeat 2 more times.
3. Grease two 12" cake pans and line them with wax paper. Fill with cake batter and bake in a preheated 350° oven for 25-30 minutes, or until a toothpick comes out clean. Turn upside down immediately onto wax paper and leave until cool. Remove cake pans and wax paper, which will have stuck to the cake.
4. Frost the two layers or slice them through their centers to create a 4-layer cake.

NOTE: This is an old-fashioned rich, heavy, delicious cake. Your company will love it!

The Best Cheesecake

5 8-ounce packages (40 ounces) Philadelphia Cream Cheese
1½ cups granulated sugar
8 eggs, separated
2 tablespoons freshly-squeezed orange juice
1 tablespoon freshly-squeezed lemon juice
1 teaspoon vanilla
½ cup sour cream
3 tablespoons all-purpose, sifted flour

1. Bring the cream cheese and the eggs to room temperature. This takes several hours.
2. Beat the cream cheese and the sugar on the highest speed of an electric mixer for 5 minutes, scraping the sides and bottom several times. Add the egg yolks and continue beating for another 5 minutes. Reduce speed to medium.
3. Add the orange and lemon juice and vanilla and continue beating for 1 minute. Add sour cream and beat for 2 more minutes. Reduce speed to low. Add flour and beat until blended only.
4. Beat egg whites in a separate bowl until soft peaks have formed and there is no moisture at the bottom of the bowl. Add 2 tablespoons sugar for a smooth consistency and beat another 20 seconds. Fold the whites into the cream cheese mixture by hand.
5. Pour into a prebaked graham cracker crust in a 9″ springform pan. Bake in a preheated 500° oven for 8 minutes, or until the top has just begun to brown. Reduce temperature to 200° and continue baking for another 50 minutes. Turn off oven. Open door. Cool in oven. Refrigerate overnight.
6. Take a knife around the edge of the springform and remove the sides. Place the cheesecake onto a cake plate and garnish with fresh strawberries or blueberries.

NOTE: I spent 20 years perfecting this easy recipe. The strawberries may be brushed with melted strawberry jelly, if you please, and the blueberries with melted apple jelly.

FOR AMARETTO CHEESECAKE: Eliminate the vanilla and use 2 teaspoons almond extract.

Doboschtorte or Genoise Batter

10 eggs
1 cup sugar
1 cup all-purpose sifted flour
1 teaspoon salt
1 teaspoon vanilla

1. Set a large earthenware (crockery) bowl over a pot of simmering water and beat the egg yolks with the sugar on the highest speed of a hand electric mixer for about 10 minutes, or until very white and mousse-like. Remove from the heat and continue beating for another 5 minutes.
2. Sift together the flour and the salt and beat into the egg mixture on low speed until blended. Add the vanilla.
3. Spoon the batter into two 10" cake pans, or three 9" cake pans. Bake at 350° on a rack ⅓ up from the bottom of the oven for 25 minutes, or until a toothpick comes out clean. Turn out. Cool. Cut the layers in halves. (You will have 6 layers from the 9" pans, or four layers from the 10" pans.)

NOTE: *a. Never overbeat flour into mixture. It makes a cake "tough."*
       b. One tablespoon rum may be added to the batter at the time of the vanilla, if desired.
       c. May be filled with chocolate mousse, rum cream filling, buttercream, or whipped cream and strawberries.
       d. Traditionally, the doboschtorte should have a thin layer of apricot or other fruit preserves spread on the bottom layer and regular fillings in the other layers.

Elizabeth's Walnut Torte

2 8" pans, well greased and floured
8 egg yolks
8 tablespoons sugar
Grated rind of ½ lemon
4 tablespoons sifted flour
8 tablespoons ground walnuts
1 teaspoon cream of tartar
8 egg whites

1. Beat yolks and sugar in a crockery bowl over simmering water with a hand electric mixer until mousse-like and full.
2. Combine lemon rind, flour and walnuts and add to egg yolk mixture.
3. Beat egg whites stiff with the cream of tartar and fold into the above mixture.
4. Pour into the cake pans, bringing the batter higher around the outside edges than in the center.
5. Bake at 350° for 30 minutes. Turn out onto wax paper and cool. Cut the layers in half.
6. Fill with butter cream filling.

NOTE: Elizabeth was our family's cook for many years. She had just arrived from Germany when she began working for us, and could not speak one word of English. She was my inspiration and mentor. I remember sitting in the kitchen as a child watching her beat the batter by hand for this marvelous torte. I never have had that kind of strength in my arms and rely upon the electric beaters for my version.

Gâteau Au Montmorency

Kirschwasser Torten

2 ounces ground almonds
4 ounces semi-sweet chocolate
5 ounces flour (⅔ cup)
6 eggs
8 ounces granulated sugar (1 cup)
10″ cake pan, greased with butter and floured
1 teaspoon arrowroot
1 16-ounce can sour, pitted cherries and their juice
1 tablespoon Kirschwasser brandy
2 pints heavy cream, whipped thick with 6 tablespoons granulated
   sugar and 2 teaspoons vanilla extract

1. Grind the almonds and put aside.
2. Melt chocolate on a covered plate over simmering water.
3. Sift the flour with a pinch of salt and set aside.
4. Put the eggs and sugar in a bowl set into a pot ½ filled with simmering water and beat them together with a hand electric mixer until very thick and mousse-like.
5. Add the melted chocolate and fold in the flour and nuts.
6. Pour into the cake pan and bake 35 minutes at 350°. Cool.
7. When the cake has cooled, cut into thirds.
8. Combine the arrowroot, cherry juice, and Kirschwasser in a small pot over a low fire and stir until thick. Add the cherries.
9. Spread the cherry mixture over the bottom layer.
10. Put the whipped cream mixture over the next layer and over the top and sides. Pipe the remaining cream into rosettes and sprinkle with chocolate shavings or curls.

Orange Chiffon Cake

2¼ cups sifted all-purpose flour
1½ cups sugar
1 tablespoon baking powder
1 teaspoon salt
½ cup vegetable oil
5 egg yolks
1 teaspoon finely-grated orange peel
¾ cup orange juice
1 teaspoon Grand Marnier liqueur
1½ teaspoons vanilla
8 egg whites
1 teaspoon cream of tartar

1. Sift together the dry ingredients into a large mixing bowl.
2. Slowly beat in the egg yolks, orange peel and juice, Grand Marnier, and vanilla.
3. Beat egg whites with cream of tartar until stiff but not dry. Pour yolk mixture into whites and fold together.
4. Pour into a 10″ tube pan.
5. Bake at 325° for 65 minutes, or until cake springs back when pressed on the top with the finger. Turn upside down onto 3 inverted cups to cool.

NOTE: May be split into 2 or 3 layers and frosted with an orange frosting, or may be served plain.

Rich Chocolate Roll

7 egg yolks
¾ cup sugar
6 tablespoons unsweetened cocoa (½ cup plus 1 tablespoon)
7 egg whites
½ teaspoon cream of tartar
¼ cup sugar

1. Preheat oven to 350°. Beat yolks and ¾ cup sugar on high speed of an electric mixer until white and mousse-like. Slowly add cocoa on lowest speed.
2. Beat egg whites until foamy. Add cream of tartar and beat until very thick. Add sugar slowly and beat on highest speed until stiff.
3. Line a large jelly roll pan (sided cookie sheet) (12″ x 17″ x 1″) with wax paper or parchment paper. Spread batter evenly. Bake 25–30 minutes. Immediately turn upside down onto a damp dish towel. Remove wax paper, trim the edges, if necessary, and roll up lengthwise while hot.

3 cups heavy cream
12 ounces semi-sweet chocolate, melted with ½ cup Crème de Cacao or Kahlua
½ cup sifted 10X confectioner's sugar

1. Beat cream very thick. Carefully beat in chocolate liqueur.
2. Unroll chocolate roll. Spread with mixture. Roll up again. Remove to a long tray. Cover thickly with mixture and pipe rosettes across the top. Refrigerate until very cold. Just before serving, sprinkle the top with powdered sugar.

Sunshine Cake

8 egg yolks, room temperature
1⅓ cups sugar
⅓ cup water
2 teaspoons vanilla
1 tablespoon orange juice
1 cup all-purpose flour, sifted
8 egg whites, room temperature
¾ teaspoon cream of tartar
Pinch of salt
½ cup mini chocolate chips (optional)
3 ounces finely-chopped pecans (optional)

1. Preheat oven to 350°.
2. Beat yolks, sugar, salt, water, vanilla, and orange juice in a bowl over simmering water with a hand electric mixer, until thick, light, and mousse-like (about 10 minutes). Remove from the heat and continue beating until cool (about 10 minutes).
3. Add flour slowly on slowest speed of hand mixer or by hand. Do not beat after flour has been blended into mixture.
4. Beat egg whites until just foamy. Add cream of tartar and salt and beat until heavy peaks have formed. Fold egg whites into batter. Stir in chocolate chips or pecans, if desired.
5. Pour into an ungreased tube pan. Put pan ⅓ up from the bottom of the oven. Bake 10 minutes at 350°. Reduce heat to 325° and bake 40 minutes more. Remove from the oven and invert pan on 3 cups which have been turned upside down. Cool completely.

NOTE: This cake is too good to frost. Serve with fresh fruit or ice cream.

Christmas Fruitcake

Makes 2 large cakes

1 cup dark brown sugar
1 cup granulated white sugar
2 cups butter (1 pound), room temperature
12 eggs, room temperature
4 cups all-purpose flour, sifted with 1 heaping teaspoon baking
  powder
¼ teaspoon mace
2 teaspoons cinnamon
1 teaspoon nutmeg
1 teaspoon ground cloves
4–5 cups, in total, of any mixture of Dromedary Fruit Mix (on the
  shelves after Thanksgiving) plus extra glacéed cherries cut into
  halves
1 cup chopped almonds
1 cup dark rum
1 cup light or golden sherry

1. Soak fruit in rum and wine conbination for 3–4 hours, turning
   occasionally with a spoon to saturate evenly.
2. Cream butter and sugar until very light (10 minutes). Add
   eggs, one at a time, on high speed. Beat 5 minutes after all eggs
   have been added.
3. Combine baking powder, cinnamon, mace, nutmeg, cloves,
   and flour. Sift into the butter/sugar/egg mixture, beating on
   low speed until just blended. Stir in the fruit and its liquors
   into the batter by hand. Stir in the nuts.
4. Pour into two well-greased or teflon bundt or ring mold pans ⅔
   full. Place pans in a pan of water (2" deep) and bake at 250° for 4
   hours.
5. Turn out of pans. Place right side up in a large round tin lined
   with aluminum foil and cheese cloth to cover. Sprinkle brandy
   and Grand Marnier combination lightly over the tops. Fold the
   cheesecloth over and put the lids on the tins. Sprinkle every
   fourth night for 2 weeks. Allow to rest for 2 more weeks at least
   before eating.

NOTE: *The longer the cake marinates, the better it is. Make 4–6 weeks before*
Christmas.

Pies and Pie Crusts

Lemon Meringue Pie

9" pie

1 baked and cooled pie crust
10½ tablespoons cornstarch
2½ cups sugar
¼ teaspoon salt
3 cups boiling water
7 jumbo or 8 large egg yolks
Reserved whites from the eggs for the meringue topping
¾ cup unstrained lemon juice

1. Sift the cornstarch and sugar and salt into a 2 quart heavy pot or the top of a double boiler. Pour the boiling water in slowly, stirring with a wooden spoon until completely blended. Cook over a medium fire, stirring constantly with the spoon and a wire whisk until smooth, thick, and creamy.
2. Beat the egg yolks with the whisk and add a bit of the hot mixture to them. Add about a cup altogether. Stir egg yolks into the pot and stir quickly until blended.
3. Pour the lemon juice into the pot very slowly, stirring well to blend. Continue cooking and stirring until very thick. Remove from top and cool completely. Do not refrigerate before spooning into baked pie shell.

Just Before Serving

Beat egg whites very thick. Add ½ cup sugar and continue beating until very stiff. Cover top of pie. Take a pastry bag and a fluted top and pipe any kind of rosettes or curly shapes around the top. Put the pie under the broiler (not too close) and watch carefully while the meringue turns brown. Serve immediately.

NOTE: This pie is only good freshly-made. If it is necessary to make the meringue in advance, I suggest dissolving 1 tablespoon (packet) unflavored gelatin in a little warm water and adding it to the egg whites when they are stiffly-beaten to hold the whites firm.

Pecan Pie

9″ deep pie plate fitted with uncooked flakey pastry crust
3 eggs
¾ cup granulated sugar
1 cup dark corn syrup
¼ cup melted butter
1½ teaspoon vanilla
2½ cups chopped pecans
36 pecan halves
1 cup heavy cream, whipped with 4 tablespoons sugar

1. Beat eggs, sugar and a pinch of salt on highest speed of an electric mixer in a crockery bowl which has been set over a pot of simmering water, until light in color and very thick (about 8–10 minutes). Remove bowl from heat and beat in corn syrup in a steady stream. Stir in melted butter and vanilla. Stir in chopped pecans.
2. Pour into the pie shell and top with the pecan halves in an attractive design (splitside down). Bake in a preheated oven at 425° for 8 minutes. Reduce heat to 325° and bake another 30 minutes, or until a knife inserted comes out clean.
3. Cool and refrigerate until very cold. Serve with whipped cream on the side.

Persian Lime Pie

A large pie to serve 10

6 ounces cream cheese, softened to room temperature
6 egg yolks
2 15-ounce cans sweetened condensed milk
1 cup freshly-squeezed lime juice

1. Beat the cream cheese with an electric beater for about 30 seconds. Add the egg yolks, one at a time, until smooth and creamy.
2. Beat in the condensed milk slowly on low speed.
3. Pour in the lime juice very slowly, beating constantly on low speed.

4. Pour into a precooked cold graham cracker crust.
5. Freeze the pie, tightly covered, until just before serving.
6. Cover with rosettes of whipped cream and decorate with thinly-sliced lime slices.

NOTE: Most recipes call it "Key Lime Pie." However, the tiny yellow Key limes are not readily available. The lime found in the stores is usually the Persian lime, and so, not to create a misnomer, the above is entitled Persian Lime Pie.

VARIATION: If you have access to my favorite fruit, the Mango, during its short season, try these two variations:

1. Either cut the amount of lime juice in half and purée ½ cup mango in a blender or –
2. Combine the following ingredients in blender:

   ¼ cup freshly-squeezed lime juice
   ¾ cup pulverized (slightly chunky) mangoes
   3 ounces cream cheese
   3 egg yolks
   1 ounce (envelope) unflavored gelatin, softened in a small amount of hot water
   1 teaspoon orange extract
   ⅛ cup Myers's dark rum
   1 15-ounce sweetened condensed milk

Follow the directions for Persian Lime Pie, but you may serve the pie from the refrigerator if you wish because of the gelatin.

CRUST VARIATION: Pulverize Oreo cookies in the food processor with enough Hershey's chocolate syrup to bind. Fit into the pie shell and freeze until ready to fill. YUMMY!

NOTE: I am convinced that the fruit which tempted Adam in the Garden of Eden was not the apple, but the mango. It is a heavenly fruit worthy of any sacrifice! Do not wait until the mango is soft to use. It is best when quite firm with good color on the skin.

Old-Fashioned Pumpkin Pie

9" pie crust, unbaked
1 cup brown sugar
½ teaspoon salt
1 teaspoon cinnamon
½ teaspoon ginger
¼ teaspoon nutmeg
¼ teaspoon allspice
¼ teaspoon cloves
1½ cups cooked or canned puréed pumpkin
3 eggs separated
1 cup sour cream

1. Line pie plate with pie dough and brush with an egg white. This keeps the dough from becoming soggy under the wet pumpkin mixture. Keep this in mind for all fruit pies also.
2. Mix dry ingredients. With a hand or electric beater, slowly beat in the pumpkin and beaten egg yolks. Slowly add sour cream until completely blended.
3. Beat egg whites until peaks form and fold them into the pumkin mixture.
4. Pour into unbaked pie shell and bake at 425° for 20 minutes. Reduce heat to 275° and bake 40 minutes more. When a knife inserted in the center comes out clean, the pie is done. Serve with sweetened whipped cream, very cold. May be covered with chopped pecans and candied chopped ginger.

Strawberry Pie

Crust

2 cups self-rising flour
½ teaspoon salt
1½ sticks plus 2 tablespoons butter, cold, cut up
⅓ cup ice water

1. Put flour, salt, butter into food processor and blend until coarse meal. Put into bowl.
2. Add water and work quickly with hands into a ball. Dust with flour. Wrap in wax paper. Chill at least one hour. Roll into a 12″ x 6″ rectangle on a floured surface. Fold into thirds (top third of rectangle over center, bottom third over the top) creating a rectangle 6″ x 4″ with open side facing you. Roll out the dough again into a 12″ x 6″ rectangle. Fold into thirds again. This completes 2 "turns." Make 2 more turns, always rolling with open side facing you.
3. Chill for 1 hour or 1 week, or put into pie plate immediately after rolling out to desired size. Bake at 350° for 10–12 minutes.

Custard

⅓ cup sugar
3½ tablespoons cornstarch
6 lightly beaten egg yolks
2 cups milk
1 teaspoon vanilla extract

1. Beat sugar, cornstarch and egg yolks with an electric mixer.
2. Warm the milk and pour it gradually over egg yolk mixture beating until smooth.
3. Pour into a pot and cook over low heat until thick and smooth. Do not allow to boil. Cool covered with a piece of wax paper.
4. Add vanilla and pour into prepared crust.
5. Melt strawberry jelly in a small saucepan and dip large strawberries (about 1 quart) individually. Place strawberries point side up on top of custard. Refrigerate several hours. Serve the same day.

Pâte Brisée

1½ cups flour
4 tablespoons softened butter
4 tablespoons solid vegetable shortening (Crisco) or very cold lard
¼ teaspoon salt
1 tablespoon sugar
1 egg yolk
2 tablespoons ice water

1. Sift the flour into a large bowl.
2. Cut up the butter and put it into the flour with the shortening, salt, sugar, and egg yolk.
3. Mix together with the hands quickly, adding the ice water slowly. Form into a ball and cover with wax paper. Refrigerate several hours.
4. Roll out onto a floured surface and set into a fluted tart casing on a greased or teflon cookie sheet. Refrigerate again or freeze for 10–15 minutes. Bake in a preheated 375° oven for ten minutes, or until golden brown. Remove sides of casing very carefully and slide Brisée onto a small serving platter. (If the sides don't remove easily from the pan, wait until the Brisée has cooled.)
5. Spoon your favorite jam all over the tart bottom just before serving. Arrange any fresh fruit in season onto the jam, and sieve powdered sugar over the top.
    Use fresh sliced peaches over apricot jam.
    Use fresh whole or sliced strawberries over strawberry jelly.
    Use kiwi fruit over apple jelly.
    Use sliced, cooked apples all by themselves, sprinkled with cinnamon-sugar.

NOTE: If the consistency of the Brisée is "mealy" when you roll it out to fit the tart casing, just piece it together. The dough should be thicker than a normal pie crust and slightly cake-like in texture.

Superb Flaky Pie Crust

¼ teaspoon baking powder
1½ cups all-purpose sifted flour
7 tablespoons butter, cut up
⅛ cup ice water

1. Put flour, baking powder, and butter into a food processor and turn on/off quickly 3 times.
2. Remove to another bowl and work with one hand while adding ice water drop by drop with the other until the dough forms a ball. Flatten slightly. Dust with flour and wrap tightly in a piece of wax paper. Chill 1 hour.
3. Roll out onto a floured board. Fit into a pie plate and refrigerate until very cold (or freeze until another time).
4. Put the cold pie crust into a preheated 375° oven and bake until light brown (about 12 minutes). Fill with Key Lime Pie, Lemon Meringue Pie, Grasshopper Pie, or Strawberry Pie.

NOTE: This recipe can be used for any baked pie as well as cold pie fillings.

Dessert Breads

Apple-Cranberry Bread

½ cup butter
1 cup sugar
1 egg
2 cups all-purpose flour
Pinch of salt
1 teaspoon baking soda
½ teaspoon cinnamon
1 cup chopped, pared tart apples, (approximately 2 medium-sized
    apples)
½ cup milk
¼ cup cranberries
¼ cup chopped walnuts

1. Cream butter and sugar until white and fluffy.
2. Add egg, beating until light.
3. Chop apples fine with cranberries and walnuts, and add to batter. (Food processor)
4. Sift flour, baking soda, salt, cinnamon into batter in 3 portions, alternating with the milk.
5. Stir batter until uniform.
6. Bake in greased bread pan at 350° for 45 minutes to 1 hour, or, until a toothpick inserted comes out "clean."
7. Cool bread in pan turned on its side until pan can be handled. Rap bottom of pan on counter and loosen bread with a knife run around the edges. Serve warm, sliced, or freeze. Defrost and reheat, covered tightly in foil, for ½ hour at 250°.

Banana Cake (Bread)

2½ cups sugar
1 cup butter, softened to room temperature
4 eggs, room temperature
2 cups bananas, puréed in blender (about 4 bananas, very ripe)
2 teaspoons vanilla
½ teaspoon almond extract
1¼ teaspoons baking soda (level)
1 teaspoon baking powder
2 cups sifted flour
8 tablespoons sour cream

1. Sift together soda, baking powder, and flour.
2. Cream butter and sugar together on highest speed of mixer until white. (Turn off the beaters occasionally to scrape the sides and bottom with a rubber spatula.)
3. Add eggs, one at a time, on medium speed until well-blended. Add vanilla and almond extract.
4. Add banana purée on medium speed until blended.
5. Beat in sour cream by the tablespoon.
6. Beat in flour mixture on low speed. Be careful not to overbeat.
7. Pour into a well-greased, or wax paper-lined 10" x 13" x 2" pan or two 8" x 8" pans to cut into squares later, and bake at 350° for 40 minutes, or until a toothpick comes out clean yet still a little "sticky."

NOTES: *This may also be baked in two loaf pans to present as banana bread. Baking time will increase to 50 minutes. You may double this recipe for the perfect gift for your friends at Christmas or when you are invited to dinner. To double: Soda will only increase to 2 teaspoons. Bananas will increase to 3¾ cups only. When you add the bananas the mixture may appear to "curdle." This will not affect taste or quality.*

VARIATION: *½ cup finely-chopped raw cranberries or ½ cup chopped walnuts may be added. Cake will take a little longer to bake. This cake freezes fantastically! You may want to defrost and heat it at 250° for 15 minutes, covered with foil.*

WARNING: *Purée bananas directly before using. Something strange happens to banana purée which has been allowed to stand.*

Banana Cake Oriental

1⅔ cups very ripe puréed bananas (in blender)
2½ cups all-purpose flour
2 teaspoons baking powder
1 teaspoon salt
¼ teaspoon ground cloves
1 teaspoon cinnamon
½ teaspoon nutmeg
1½ sticks butter (12 tablespoons)
1 cup sugar
2 eggs, beaten

1. Combine the flour, baking powder, soda, salt, and spices and sift. Set aside.
2. Cream the butter and sugar until white and fluffy. Add the eggs, one at a time, beating until well-blended. Puree the bananas in a blender and slowly add them to the mixture.
3. Add the flour mixture into the wet ingredients by thirds, mixing gently with a wire whisk until just blended and smooth. Do not beat or flour will toughen, making the cake heavy.
4. Pour into two well-greased 8" layer cake pans and bake at 350° for 30 minutes. Test with a toothpick. It should have just a hint of dry batter stuck to it.
5. Turn out upside down immediately to cool. Frost with a thin layer of orange marmalade inside and out or with a white frosting. Grand Marnier may be sprinkled over the marmalade sparingly for a declicious flavor.

NOTE: I freeze these to serve for unexpected company. Peaches or mangoes may be substituted for bananas. Add the juice of ½ lime.

Orange Nut Bread

3 cups flour
3 teaspoons baking powder
½ teaspoon salt
¼ cup sugar

1. Sift together and set aside for later.

   ½ cup chopped walnuts
   1 tablespoon grated orange rind
   ½ cup orange marmalade
   2 tablespoons fresh orange juice
   1 egg, beaten
   1 cup milk

1. Stir into the flour mixture and mix well. Put into a well-greased loaf pan. Allow to stand for 10 minutes. Bake at 350° for ¾ hour.
2. Slice and spread with cream cheese and orange marmalade or butter for breakfast. Or serve at luncheon or on the buffet table.

Pumpkin Bread

A big loaf

2 cups sugar
1 cup butter
4 eggs
1 16-ounce can pumpkin pulp

1. Beat the sugar and the shortening until smooth and creamy.
2. Add the eggs to the sugar mixture, one at a time, on medium speed, beating well after each addition. Add the pumpkin, beating until blended.

3 cups all-purpose pre-sifted flour
2 teaspoons cinnamon
1 teaspoon nutmeg
1½ teaspoon salt
½ teaspoon ground cloves
¼ teaspoon ground ginger
⅛ teaspoon ground mace
1¼ teaspoons baking powder

1. Sift the flour and the spices and baking powder together.
2. Add ½ of the flour mixture to the other mixture. Slowly add ¼ cup cool water, beating on low speed. Add the rest of the flour and another ¼ cup water, beating only until blended. (Do not overbeat.)
3. Pour into a well-greased loaf pan and bake in a preheated 350° oven for 1 hour 10 minutes. Turn out onto an oblong cake dish. Serve for breakfast, or with ice cream as a dessert.

NOTE: *This may also be made with 2 cups coarsely-grated carrots instead of the pumpkin pulp.*

Raisin Gingerbread

⅓ cup molasses
⅓ cup dark Karo syrup
⅔ cup sugar
⅔ cup boiling water
2 tablespoons melted butter
1 teaspoon baking soda
1 egg, beaten
½ cup raisins
½ cup chopped walnuts
1½ cups sifted flour
1 teaspoon cinnamon
1 teaspoon ginger

1. Combine molasses, Karo syrup, sugar, boiling water, butter, and baking soda in a mixing bowl. Stir together and cool. Add raisins and nuts and egg. Stir.
2. Sift together the flour, cinnamon and ginger and stir into the molasses mixture.
3. Pour batter into an oiled 9" pan, or gingerbread pan mold. Bake in moderate oven (350°) for 35–40 minutes. Turn out immediately so it will not stick.

Frostings 'n' Fillings

Rum Cream Filling

For Doboschtorte

1 tablespoon (1 envelope) unflavored gelatin
3 tablespoons cold water
¾ cup light rum
4 cups heavy cream
¾ cup 10X confectioner's sugar, sifted
1 teaspoon vanilla extract

1. Sprinkle the gelatin over the water in a small heatproof cup and allow to stand 5 minutes. Stir in ¼ cup of the rum. Place cup in hot water until the gelatin is dissolved. Remove from heat.
2. In a large bowl beat cold cream, sugar, vanilla, and the remainder of the rum almost thick. Beat in the gelatin. Do not overbeat or cream will curdle. Beat only to the very thick stage.
3. Turn first layer of cake upside down on the cake platter and spread the filling in a thin layer all the way to the edge, but not over. Place the next layer on top and spread the cream. Continue until all layers are filled, leaving the top and sides bare. Cool in the refrigerator with a piece of wax paper covering the top so it won't harden. When filling has set (about 1 hour), cover the top and sides with a chocolate frosting.

Strawberry Filling

For Chocolate Doboschtorte without flour

2 pints fresh strawberries, washed, hulled and sliced
1 16-ounce bag frozen strawberries in sweet syrup
2 tablespoons arrowroot thickener

1. Defrost frozen strawberries and put into a blender with their juice. Blend on high until smooth and thick. Pour into a saucepan with arrowroot and cook on medium heat, stirring with a wooden spoon until thick. Do not allow to boil.
2. Cool and fold fresh berries into the sauce and fill cake layers.

Chocolate Buttercream Filling and Frosting

½ pound unsalted butter
1 pound 10X confectioner's sugar, sifted (if food processor is used, it is not necessary to sift)
1 egg
1 egg yolk
6 ounces semi-sweet chocolate
2 ounces unsweetened chocolate
1 teaspoon vanilla

1. Cream butter and sugar until light in color and consistency.
2. Add egg and egg yolk, beating until blended.
3. Melt chocolate in a double boiler. Add vanilla. Do not stir. Cool.
4. Pour cooled chocolate mixture into the egg mixture and pour into butter mixture, mixing thoroughly.
5. Frost. If frosting is too loose, refrigerate for 10 minutes.

Food Processor Method

1. Cut butter into pieces and put in food processor. Turn on for 5 seconds. Scrape sides.
2. Add sugar, turn on again for 5 seconds. Scrape sides. Turn on until white and fluffy.
3. Add egg and egg yolk and turn on for just a second.
4. This mixture must then be stirred into the chocolate by hand.

Rum Icing

½ pound butter
1 pound 10X confectioner's sugar, sifted
½ cup dark rum

1. Cream butter. Gradually add sugar and rum.
2. Spread on cake and sprinkle with crushed macaroons.

Filling for Layer Cakes

8 ounces semi-sweet chocolate
4 ounces unsweetened chocolate
½ pound butter (unsalted)
1⅓ cups confectioner's sugar
4 egg yolks
1 tablespoon vanilla extract
6 tablespoons dark rum
1 pint heavy cream for whipping

1. Melt the chocolate with the vanilla and rum.
2. Cream the butter and sugar on high speed of an electric mixer. Add the egg yolks and beat until well-blended.
3. Beat in the chocolate.
4. In a separate bowl beat the cream until very thick. Fold it into the chocolate mixture.
5. Refrigerate mixture for ½ hour and then fill layers and cover top and sides of 7 layer cake. Sprinkle chopped hazelnuts over top and sides. Refrigerate until ready to serve.

Grand Marnier Frosting

½ cup sifted confectioner's sugar
¼ cup orange juice
⅓ cup Grand Marnier liqueur
¼ cup orange marmalade

1. Bring to a boil and pour slowly over cake, letting the juice drip down the sides at random.

The Inebriated Mousse

Sober Chocolate Angel Mousse

9"–10" springform pan
1 large angel food cake
10 ounces semi-sweet chocolate
4 ounces unsweetened chocolate
2 teaspoons vanilla
4 egg yolks
2 pints heavy cream for the inside
1½ pints heavy cream for the outside
½ cup granulated sugar

1. Melt chocolate with the vanilla in a double boiler. Set aside to cool. Stir in the egg yolks, which have been beaten smooth.
2. Put 2 pints heavy cream into a large bowl and whip until very thick. Stir a few tablespoons of the whipped cream into the chocolate. Stir the chocolate into the whipped cream until well-blended.
3. Break the angel food cake into irregular chunks about 2"–3" in size and fold them carefully together until completely coated by the chocolate mixture. Spoon loosely into the springform pan. Refrigerate overnight.
4. In the morning, remove the sides of the springform and set the cake onto a large cake platter. Beat the 1½ pints heavy cream until very thick. Slowly add the sugar and continue beating until incorporated. Cover the top and sides of the cake heavily. Pipe rosettes all over the top with the remaining cream, using a fluted piping tube. Shave semi-sweet chocolate or make chocolate curls and decorate the top heavily. Refrigerate until serving.

NOTE: This is a gorgeous cake and everybody's favorite dessert for the holidays. If you use it as a buffet item it is necessary to add gelatin to hold it up. Combine one tablespoon (packet) unflavored gelatin with ¼ cup lukewarm water to dissolve and stir it into your melted chocolate.

Frangelico or Amaretto Mousse

Serves 2 people

3 egg yolks
¼ cup sugar
1 pint heavy cream
4 ounces Frangelico or Amaretto Liqueur
3 egg whites
½ cup toasted, chopped almonds for Amaretto or toasted chopped
   hazelnuts for Frangelico
Lady Fingers
½ quart glass soufflé dish

1. Beat the egg yolks and sugar in a bowl over simmering water until very thick.
2. In another bowl beat the heavy cream until almost thick. Slowly pour in the liqueur while beating very thick.
3. In a separate bowl, beat the egg whites until thick, adding 1 tablespoon sugar at the end just to smooth.
4. Fold the 3 mixtures together.
5. Split the lady fingers down the center and arrange around the soufflé dish. Spoon in the mousse. Sprinkle the nuts over the top and refrigerate several hours or overnight.

NOTE: For a stronger flavor, add ½ teaspoon almond extract to the Amaretto mousse.

Raspberry Mousse

1 cup frozen raspberries and their juice (1 10-ounce package),
    defrosted
2 tablespoons Maraschino liqueur
2 tablespoons Chambord liqueur
1 tablespoon unflavored gelatin (1 package)
3 egg whites, room temperature
1 tablespoon sugar
1 pint heavy cream for whipping, very cold

1. Make a collar 2" deep from wax paper and tape it around a 1 quart soufflé dish.
2. Soften the gelatin in ¼ cup warm water and stir in the liqueurs. Stir in the raspberries and their juice.
3. Beat the egg whites until stiff and add the sugar, beating until just smooth.
4. Whip the cream stiff.
5. Fold the cream into the raspberry mixture.
6. Fold in the egg whites.
7. Spoon into the soufflé dish and refrigerate several hours.
8. Take a sharp knife and run it around the inside of the paper collar before removing it.
9. Serve with fresh raspberries on the side.

Strawberry Mousse

3 pints fresh strawberries
2 tablespoons unflavored gelatin
½ cup lukewarm water
Juice of ½ lemon
1⅓ cup 10X confectioner's sugar
3 pints heavy cream for whipping, very cold
2 tablespoons red currant jelly
2 drops red food coloring
½ cup Kirsch liqueur
2½ quart bundt mold or jello mold

1. Slice 2 pints of the strawberries and pour the lemon juice over them.
2. Soften gelatin in ½ cup lukewarm water and place the cup in hot water.
3. Whip the cream with the sugar and vanilla until very thick. Reserve ½ pint.
4. Add the currant jelly and food coloring. Beat the gelatin in slowly until well-blended. Stir in the Kirsch.
5. Stir in the strawberries.
6. Spoon into the oiled mold. Refrigerate overnight, or for several hours. Unmold by inserting a knife around outside edge and inside tube to loosen. Turn upside down on a serving plate and allow to stand for 10 minutes. Mold should slide out easily. Fill the center with 1 pint sliced strawberries and decorate with rosettes of whipped cream piped through a fluted tube.

NOTE: *This mousse may also be put into a 2 quart soufflé dish after creating a "collar" of wax paper to pile it high. Decorate with whole strawberries on the top.*

The Hot Soufflé

The Soufflé

When I am laid to my worldly rest
Remember me not for my sauce's zest,
Not for my cruller haughtily-puffed,
Nor for my omelet, layered, and fluffed.

When I am laid to my worldly rest
Remember I passed the Ultimate Test
Of Cheese and Chocolate and Grand Marnier
When I created the perfect Soufflé.

Valerie Hart

Cheese Soufflé

2 tablespoons butter
2 tablespoons flour
¾ cup milk
Pinch of salt and pinch of cayenne pepper
4 egg yolks
6 egg whites
½ cup grated Parmesan cheese
½ cup grated Swiss cheese

1. Melt butter in a saucepan over medium heat. Stir in the flour and blend well. Stir in milk, which has been warmed, and season with a pinch of salt and cayenne pepper.
2. Remove the saucepan from the fire and stir in egg yolks after mixture has cooled a bit. Stir in grated cheeses. Return to a low fire and stir until the cheese has melted and well blended with other ingredients. Remove from heat, cover with wax paper, and allow to sit at room temperature until directly before cooking.
3. Directly before cooking, beat egg whites stiff with 1 heaping teaspoon cream of tartar. Fold into the cheese mixture. Pour into a 1-quart soufflé dish, which has been rubbed with butter and dusted with fine breadcrumbs.
4. Bake at 375° for about 30 minutes, or until the top is well-browned. Serve at once.

NOTE: If you add a bit of the whites first to the cheese and stir and then fold the rest into the cheese, it will "loosen" the mixture making it easier to combine.

Crabmeat Soufflé

Serves 4 people as a first course or 2 people for luncheon

4 tablespoons butter
3 tablespoons flour
1 cup hot milk
Pinch of salt, white pepper, nutmeg and cayenne pepper
1 tablespoon lemon juice (fresh)
1 cup shredded cooked crabmeat
4 egg yolks, lightly beaten
6 egg whites
¼ cup grated Romano cheese

1. Melt butter. Stir in flour, and gradually add the milk, stirring constantly with a wooden spoon and a wire whisk until the sauce is smooth and thick.
2. Stir in the salt, pepper, nutmeg and cayenne. Stir in the lemon juice. Add a little of this mixture to the beaten egg yolks and then stir the egg yolks back into the mixture. Stir in the cheese. Remove from the heat and cool, covered with wax paper.
3. Just before placing in the oven beat the egg whites stiff with ⅛ teaspoon cream of tartar. Rub butter all around a one quart soufflé dish. Sprinkle a tablespoon of fine bread crumbs into the dish and shake them around to adhere to the butter. Fold the egg whites into the other mixture and spoon into the soufflé dish. Bake in a preheated 350° oven for 35–40 minutes. Serve immediately.

Vanilla Sauce

2 cups heavy cream
2 eggs
2 egg yolks
¼ cup sugar
1½ tablespoons vanilla

1. In a saucepan, combine cream, eggs, egg yolks, sugar and beat the mixture with a whisk over moderate heat until it coats a spoon. Stir in the vanilla. This is a slow process. Do not allow to boil. Use a wire whisk and a wooden spoon alternately to stir sauce.

2. Strain into a serving bowl and chill. (Makes 2½ cups.)

NOTE: *May be made 2-3 days in advance.*

VARIATION: *½ cup heavy cream, whipped thick, may be stirred in directly before serving. ¼ cup Amaretto or Grand Marnier, or ⅛ cup light rum makes a delightful variation. Serve with chocolate or vanilla soufflé.*

Chocolate Soufflé

Serves 6 people

4½ tablespoons butter
2 tablespoons flour
1½ cups warm milk
4 ounces semi-sweet chocolate
¼ teaspoon salt
½ cup sugar
2 teaspoons vanilla extract
6 egg yolks
8 egg whites
½ teaspoon cream of tartar

1. Melt the butter in a saucepan. Add the flour, stirring until dissolved.
2. Gradually add the milk, stirring constantly with a wooden spoon and a wire whisk over a low fire.
3. Add the chocolate, salt, and sugar and continue to cook, stirring until well-blended and thick. Remove from the fire. Stir a bit of the hot chocolate into the egg yolks and then the yolks into the pot of chocolate. Add the vanilla and return to the fire. Cook, stirring for another minute. Remove from fire, cover tightly with wax paper, and allow to sit at room temperature until ready to bake. (This portion may be made in the morning.)
4. Just before baking, beat egg whites stiff with the cream of tartar. Fold the whites into the chocolate in a large bowl.
5. Butter and sprinkle granulated sugar around the entire inside of a 4-quart soufflé dish. Pour in the batter, pushing it higher around the sides than in the middle. Bake on the bottom rack of the oven at 375° for 45 minutes. Serve immediately with vanilla sauce on the side.

Raspberry Soufflé

Light and delicious
Serves 4 people

⅔ cup puréed raspberries
4 tablespoons Framboise liqueur (or Chambord)
2 egg yolks
2 tablespoons sugar
4 egg whites
1 teaspoon cream of tartar
1 teaspoon sugar

1. Bring eggs to room temperature.
2. Push the raspberries through a strainer or sieve to remove seeds. (If you are using frozen raspberries, drain off all liquid.)
3. Add liqueur to raspberry purée.
4. Beat egg yolks and sugar in a bowl over simmering water with a hand electric mixer until thick and mousse-like. Slowly beat in raspberry purée. Remove from heat.
5. Beat egg whites and cream of tartar until very thick and add 1 teaspoon sugar at the end just to smooth it out for easier folding.
6. Fold the egg whites into the raspberry mixture by hand with a spatula.
7. Pour into a 1-quart soufflé dish, which has been rubbed with butter and sprinkled all over the inside with sugar.
8. Bake on the bottom rack of an electric oven, or on the floor of a gas oven, preheated at 375°, for 20 minutes.
9. Serve with fresh raspberries, if available.

Crêpes

Basic Rules for Making Successful Crêpes

1. Do not double the recipe for the batter. Make as many times as you please, but separately.
2. Never overcook a crêpe. It will become brittle and break when you are trying to fold it later.
3. When making fillings for the luncheon crêpes, make your sauce thicker than you normally would so it will not "run" out of the crêpe.
4. Always allow the batter to stand at room temperature for at least 1 hour. Then beat again (strain if lumpy) and pour into a handled cup. (A measuring cup is the best.)
5. Any pan (4" for dessert and hors d'oeuvres, 5" for luncheon or dinner) can become a crêpe pan. The new crêpe makers are fun to use, but not actually necessary for a successful crêpe. Teflon pans are excellent and need not be "seasoned."
6. If pan is not coated with a Teflon substance, "season" it by taking a piece of brown paper (from a grocery bag) and, rubbing sweet butter into it, rub the pan well all over with the paper. Put the pan on a medium fire and, when it is quite hot, make a thick pancake from the batter. Discard it (or eat it). Season the pan once again, and make crêpes. No more greasing of the pan should be necessary.
7. To freeze: Cover tightly and freeze. Thaw completely before trying to pull apart to fill.

To Make Crêpes

1. Season pan, if necessary.
2. Put pan on medium fire and allow to become hot.
3. Hold the handle of the pan with one hand and pour batter from measuring cup into hot pan. Batter will adhere to pan. Immediately remove pan from heat and pour excess batter back into cup. Return pan to fire.
4. Cook until light brown on one side. Remove by loosening edge with a knife and pulling crêpe out of pan with fingers.
5. Allow to cool on a dish towel. Stack.
6. The filled crêpe freezes beautifully.

To Fill Crêpes

1. The browned side becomes the inside of the crêpe.
2. Lay crêpe on table. Put 1 large tablespoon of filler into center of the circle.
3. To create an oblong for the luncheon or dinner crêpe, fold only two edges inward, making sure one completely overlaps the other so the mixture is concealed. To create a square blintz, fold the four edges inward, moving around the circle, to create an envelope which will hold together in the cooking.
4. Cook, flap side down first, in both cases, to seal.
5. You may fry filled crêpes in butter or margarine, until golden brown; or, you may bake them on a greased cookie sheet at 350° after brushing them with butter.

Crêpes for Chicken or Seafood

1½ cups flour, sifted
½ teaspoon salt
3 eggs, beaten
1½ cups milk or chicken broth

1. Sift the flour and the salt into a bowl. Beat the eggs separately and pour them into the flour. Pour milk in slowly, beating constantly with a wire whisk.
2. When mixture is well-blended, strain into a cup with a pouring spout.
3. Make crêpes in a 6" pan.

Seafood Filling for Crêpes or Phyllo Dough

20 crêpes

2 pounds of any mixture of shrimp, lobster, scallops, cut into
    coarse pieces
4 tablespoons butter
3 tablespoons flour
2 cups milk (if you like it richer add 1 cup milk and 1 cup cream)
½ teaspoon white pepper
½ teaspoon salt
2 tablespoons dill weed (fresh), or 1 tablespoon dried dill
1 teaspoon mustard
½ lemon, squeezed
½ pound mushrooms, sliced
½ cup Romano cheese, grated

1. Melt butter. Add flour, stirring until blended. Slowly add hot milk and cream, stirring constantly until thick and smooth.
2. Add seasonings. Add shrimp or scallops and cook on a slow fire until "just" done. Do not overcook, or seafood will become tough. (Lobster must be precooked before adding. It takes 15 minutes to boil a lobster.)
3. In a separate pan sauté the mushrooms in a little butter or margarine until soft. Pour off liquid and add them to the seafood.
4. Fill crêpes, sprinkling grated Romano cheese over the filling before folding into oblong shapes. Fry in butter or bake at 350° on a greased cookie sheet after brushing each crêpe with melted butter.

NOTE: *Phyllo dough may be filled with this recipe. Follow the instructions on the box for filling and cooking. Allow to cool for 10 minutes before slicing into pieces.*

Crêpes for Cheese Blintzes

1½ cups self-rising flour
1½ cups milk
1 teaspoon salt
1 tablespoon sugar
4 beaten eggs

1. Mix the flour, salt, sugar, and eggs. Add the milk slowly, beating with an old-fashioned egg beater, wire whisk, or hand electric beater until completely blended. Cover with wax paper and allow to stand on the kitchen counter for 1 hour.
2. Beat again until blended. Strain into a measuring cup with a handle.
3. Heat crêpe pan after "seasoning" on a medium high fire, and cook crêpes.
4. Prepare Filling for Cheese Blintzes. Fill crêpes. Cook.

NOTE: See "Basic Rules for Making Successful Crêpes."

Filling for Cheese Blintzes

8 ounces Farmer's cheese
8 ounces cream cheese
2 egg yolks
1 whole egg
2 tablespoons sugar
Pinch of salt
¼ teaspoon cinnamon
⅛ teaspoon nutmeg

1. Combine ingredients and beat until smooth. Spoon a bit onto the center of each crêpe. Tightly roll up crêpes, folding in the ends first so the cheese won't ooze out.
2. Fry in unsalted butter on a medium fire until golden brown, or bake on a greased cookie sheet at 350°, after brushing tops with melted unsalted butter.
3. Serve with sour cream and fresh fruit on the side for dipping. May be kept hot on an electric platter.

Apple Filling for Dessert Crêpes

6 Rome apples, peeled and cut into small squares
⅓ cup sugar
1 teaspoon cinnamon
2 teaspoons flour
2 teaspoons Grand Marnier
½ cup butter
½ cup Grand Marnier to flame

1. Combine sugar, cinnamon and flour in a cup.
2. Sauté the apples in the butter until they are soft, stirring often to absorb the butter. Sprinkle the sugar mixture over them, stirring until completely mixed. Sprinkle with the 2 teaspoons Grand Marnier and toss.
3. Fill the dessert crêpes and fold one flap over the other, creating an oblong.
4. Place into a pan which may be brought to the table.
5. Pour ½ cup hot Grand Marnier over the crêpes and ignite with a match. Serve the minute the flame subsides, spooning the juice over the crêpes.

Jam Crêpe

1 tablespoon flour
½ teaspoon sugar
1 egg
¼ teaspoon vanilla
1 tablespoon milk
1 tablespoon thick jam of your choice

1. Mix the flour, sugar, egg, vanilla, and milk together and pour into a 6″ round crêpe or Teflon-coated pan over medium heat. Spoon jam onto one half of the pancake. Allow the bottom to set and fold the half without jam over the other with a spatula. Serve with a sprinkling of powdered sugar and treat yourself to happiness!

Crêpes Suzette

1¼ cups sifted all-purpose flour
4 eggs
4 egg yolks
1 quart milk
2 teaspoons sugar
1 teaspoon salt
1 tablespoon Grand Marnier brandy

1. Mix the flour, eggs, and egg yolks on slow speed of a hand electric mixer. Add the salt, sugar, brandy and slowly pour in the milk, beating slowly and scraping around the sides occasionally with a rubber spatula. Cover and allow to stand at room temperature for 1 hour.
2. Heat a 4″ skillet and brush it with unsalted clarified butter, or use a Teflon pan.
3. Beat the crêpe batter slightly and pour it into a cup equipped with a pouring spout.
4. Pour some batter into the hot skillet and quickly tilt and rotate the pan so the liquid covers the entire bottom. Pour off any batter in excess of that which adheres to the bottom of the pan. Cook the crêpe quickly on both sides, and remove to a piece of wax paper or toweling to cool. Repeat the process until all are cooked, stacking them as they cool. Cover with wax paper and reserve for later.

NOTE: These may be put into an air-tight container or plastic bag and frozen.

Sauce for Crêpes Suzette

Yields 8 crêpes—Serves 4 people

4 large lumps white sugar
1 orange
2 drops lemon juice
3 tablespoons unsalted butter, plus ¼ cup clarified butter
1 ounce Maraschino liqueur (Optional)
1 ounce cognac or brandy (Martel or Remy Martin or Couvoisier)
1 ounce Curaçao
¼ cup Grand Marnier

1. Rub both sides of the lump sugar hard on the orange skin until they have taken in the flavor.
2. Cream three tablespoons butter with the sugar on a flat plate by mashing them together with a fork.
3. Pour the clarified butter into a flat skillet or chafing dish or proper French copper-bottom crêpe pan, which has been set over a butane or alcohol or Sterno stove. (Réchaud) Squeeze the juice from the orange into the dish. Add the lemon.
4. Add the sugar/orange mixture.
5. Add half of the Grand Marnier. Stir with a spoon over a high flame until very hot.
6. Add the Maraschino, brandy, Caraçao, and remaining Grand Marnier and allow to become very hot and bubbly. Light a match to it. (Carefully!)
7. Take the crêpes, one at a time, with a fork and a spoon (this takes some practice to look professional) and soak them in the sauce as you fold them into quarters, or into halves with one side overlapping the other. As each crêpe is folded, push it to the side of the pan, forming a row, until all the crêpes are finished. Spoon the hot sauce over the entire batch and serve immediately.

NOTE: *Steps #1–#4 may be done in advance to expedite the dinner show.*

Old-Fashioned Belgian Waffles

1½ cups flour
2 teaspoons baking powder
1 teaspoon baking soda
3 teaspoons sugar
½ teaspoon salt
2 eggs, separated
2 cups sour cream
4 tablespoons melted butter
1 teaspoon vanilla extract
1 tablespoon orange juice

1. Mix together dry ingredients.
2. Beat egg whites until thick and peaks form but not stiff.
3. Mix egg yolks, sour cream, melted butter, and vanilla.
4. Mix wet ingredients with dry ingredients until just blended.
5. Stir in egg whites. Cover bowl and allow to stand for 15 minutes.
6. Spoon onto a hot Belgian waffle maker. (Round) Serve with powdered sugar, jam, maple syrup and fresh fruit with link sausages and bacon. Or, serve them in the afternoon with a scoop of vanilla ice cream and chocolate sauce!

NOTE: I make these up in advance and freeze them to be reheated when the waffle mood hits people.

Miscellaneous Desserts

Cream Puffs (Pâte-à-Chou)

Food processor method

1 scant cup water
¼ teaspoon salt
¼ pound butter
1 scant cup flour
3 large eggs

1. Bring the water, salt and butter to a boil. When butter has completely dissolved, remove from heat and quickly pour in the flour all at once. Stir hard, bringing the ingredients together into a large ball at the side of the pot and allow to cool for 10 minutes.
2. Put the ball of dough into the food processor with the steel blade and turn on for just a second. Turn off and add the three eggs all at once. Turn on and leave on for 10 seconds. Turn off. Turn on again for another 10 seconds. Turn off.
3. Spoon batter onto a cookie sheet, which has been covered with a sheet of waxed paper. Release the mounds of batter from the teaspoon with your index finger, bring each into a peak.
4. Bake in a preheated 350° oven about 20–30 minutes, or until puffed and brown. Remove from the oven. Allow to cool for about 10 minutes and split the puffs in halves horizontally to allow the air to escape.
5. Freeze for later in an airtight container or fill with cheese or mushroom or seafood filling for hors d'oeuvre. If you make them larger you may fill them with chicken salad or chicken a la king for lunch. If you add 1 teaspoon sugar to the water at the beginning you have dessert Profiterole to be filled with sweetened whipped cream or creme patisserie.

NOTE: This recipe should yield about 40 puffs. When you have to beat the eggs in by hand this is a lengthy and difficult recipe. When I devised the food processor method I was ecstatic how easy and foolproof this wonderful curiosity of cooking had become. I make them by the hundreds and freeze them for unexpected company.

Crème Brûlée

1 pint heavy cream
6 egg yolks
½ cup sugar
2 teaspoons vanilla
1 quart shallow baking dish

1. Heat cream almost to the boiling point but do not allow to boil. Remove from stove.
2. Beat egg yolks and sugar until blended with an electric mixer or wire whisk. Pour the hot cream over them very slowly, mixing in well.
3. Add the vanilla and beat about 10 seconds longer. Pour into the baking dish. Set the dish into a pan of water 1" deep and bake at 350° for 45 minutes, or until a knife inserted comes out "clean." Remove from the water and cool at room temperature.
4. Sprinkle the entire top well with granulated sugar about ⅛" thick. Put under the broiler and broil until brown and bubbly but not burned. Cool and chill very cold.
5. Serve with sweetened whipped cream or chocolate sauce on the side. However, it's also marvelous plain.

NOTE: Recipe may be doubled for a crowd.

English Trifle

A very special dessert

1 16-ounce can pitted bing cherries
¾ cup Harvey's Bristol Cream Sherry
Large glass bowl
A double recipe of light pastry cream
1 Sunshine Cake (Or, if you don't have time, a good store-bought
   sponge cake)
Raspberry Jam
1 29-ounce can sliced freestone style peaches
Thinly sliced almonds

1. Drain the cherries and marinate them in the sherry several
   hours.
2. Make the Pastry Cream (page 240) and allow it to cool.
3. Slice ¾ of the cake ½" in thickness and line the bottom and half-
   way up the sides of the glass bowl.
4. Spread a thin layer of raspberry jam over each slice.
5. Drain the peaches and dry them on paper toweling. Set them
   over the jam, reserving 6–8 for the top.
6. Cover with ½ of the pastry cream.
7. Slice the rest of the cake and put it on top of the pastry cream.
   Sprinkle well with all the sherry from the cherries and set the
   cherries on top evenly.
8. Cover with the rest of the pastry cream.
9. Sprinkle the nuts on top and decorate with the reserved peach
   slices. Cover tightly with plastic wrap and refrigerate. Serve
   very cold.

NOTE: The beauty of this dessert is looking into the glass bowl.

Light Pastry Cream for Cream Puffs, Trifle or Custard Pies

½ cup sugar
5 egg yolks (6, if not the largest size)
3½ tablespoons cornstarch
Pinch of salt
2 cups milk
1 teaspoon vanilla (or, more to taste)
½ cup heavy cream, whipped thick

1. Beat sugar, salt, egg yolks, and cornstarch with an electric beater, pouring in the milk slowly until well-blended.
2. Pour into a pot over a medium fire and stir with a wooden spoon until the mixture begins to thicken. Stir well with a wire whisk to remove any lumps. Continue stirring with your wooden spoon until mixture is very thick. Remove from fire. Stir in the vanilla. Cover tightly with a top or wax paper and cool completely. (Do not refrigerate.)
3. Whip the cream and fold it into the custard. Fill pastry puffs or use as a base for Trifle or custard pies.

NOTE: *For chocolate pastry cream, stir in 2 tablespoons unsweetened cocoa and 1 teaspoon strong coffee with the cornstarch during step #1.*

This is a foolproof technique. When you do the whole process in the pot you easily have a lumpy custard. My way insures you of a smooth custard made the simple way.

Incredible Chocolate Sauce

1 tablespoon vanilla
4 ounces unsweetened chocolate
4 tablespoons unsalted butter
1½ cups granulated sugar
¾ cup whole milk
¾ cup heavy cream

1. Melt the chocolate and vanilla and butter over low heat. Slowly stir in the milk and cream over medium heat. Stir in the sugar and cook, stirring occasionally, over medium-low heat for ½ hour. Serve hot or cold.

NOTE: Perfect over Profiterole (Cream Puffs).

Chocolate Zabaglione

3 ounces semi-sweet chocolate
2 tablespoons cream, room temperature
4 egg yolks, room temperature
¼ cup sugar
½ cup Marsala wine (or Port)
Whipped cream, sweetened with vanilla extract and sugar

1. Melt chocolate. Remove from heat and stir in cream. Set aside.
2. Put the sugar and egg yolks in a bowl and beat with a wire whisk or electric hand beater until white and thick. Add wine slowly and continue beating for 5 minutes. Slowly pour in the chocolate cream and beat another minute.
3. Serve in stem glasses and top with whipped cream, or, layer the chocolate mixture with the whipped cream mixture, dotting the tops with rosettes of cream piped through a piping tube.

NOTE: Best when beaten in a copper bowl.

Zucotto

2 ounces slivered almonds or chopped hazelnuts
1 cup chopped glacéed fruit mix
4 ounces chopped glacéed cherries
1 quart good vanilla ice cream
2 pints heavy cream
10 ounces semi-sweet chocolate
1 cup sifted 10X confectioner's sugar
1 12-inch sponge cake, Sunshine Cake (page 187) or Lady Fingers
1 cup brandy mixed with 1½ cups Amaretto, Frangelico or Kahlua

1. Line a stainless bowl or zucotto mold with cheesecloth, hanging it over the edges for easy removal later.
2. Slice the cake into ¼" thick pieces diagonally and sprinkle liqueur over.
3. Line the mold with the cake points at the bottom.
4. Bring the ice cream to the soft stage and stir in the fruits. Stir in 2 tablespoons of the liqueur. Spoon it into the mold, bringing it up to the top of the cake along the sides leaving a large hole in the center. Freeze for ½ hour.
5. Press slivered almonds or hazelnuts all over the ice cream.
6. Whip cream thick and slowly add sugar, whipping until incorporated. Melt the chocolate and beat it into the cream when slightly cooled. Fill the center of the mold.
7. Cover the top of the mold with cake slices and sprinkle with liqueur. Cover the top with foil and freeze for several hours, or overnight.
8. Remove from freezer and pull the zucotto out of the mold by the cheesecloth "tails." Turn out onto a serving platter. Remove the cheesecloth. Allow to stand at room temperature 15 minutes before cutting.

NOTE: *The fruit is the same as you would use in a Christmas fruit cake. It is not always available, so buy enough at Christmas time and store in a cool place. This cake may be frozen for several weeks. Make a few small ones to have available for unexpected company.*

Sugared Grapes

2 bunches seedless grapes: the largest available (about 1 pound)
1 egg white
1 cup granulated sugar

1. Beat the egg white with a fork until frothy. Dip the grapes into it until well-coated. Cover heavily with the sugar and set onto a platter. Serve as a dessert or as an accompaniment to fish or a luncheon dish.

NOTE: *Do not refrigerate! The dampness of the refrigerator will make the sugar break down. However, they are incredible frozen!*

Sugared Pecans

4 tablespoons butter
1 pound pecans, shelled and halved
½ cup white sugar
1 tablespoon white corn syrup

1. Melt butter in a large skillet.
2. Toss pecans in it until completely coated.
3. Sprinkle sugar over nuts and toss well.
4. Dribble corn syrup and continue tossing.
5. Spread onto a cookie sheet and bake at 150–200° for 45 minutes, or until sugar and nuts are dry and crunchy.

NOTE: *These pecans are superlative. They make a marvelous hors d'oeuvres. However, one should really eat them while sitting in front of a mirror. If you consume enough you can watch yourself grow larger while you eat.*

Phyllo Chocolate Nutties

4 ounces walnuts, broken into small pieces
2 ounces almonds, broken into small pieces
3 sheets phyllo dough
Honey to bind (about 3 tablespoons or more)
2 ounces unsweetened good quality cocoa
2 ounces powdered sugar
2 tablespoons unsalted butter to brush over for baking

1. Combine the nuts, honey, cocoa, and powdered sugar.
2. Take 3 sheets of the phyllo dough and pile them on top of each other. Spread the mixture over the top sheet. Roll up jellyroll style. Cut into 1" pieces but do not separate. Brush the top and sides with the melted butter and bake about 25 minutes at 375° or until brown.

Blanche's Rice Pudding

½ cup long-grained white rice (Uncle Ben's)
1½ cups water to cook it in
4 eggs, beaten with a pinch of salt
1 quart milk
1 cup sugar
2½ ounces black seedless raisins (½ cup)

1. Cook rice in the water, covered, until tender.
2. Beat eggs with a pinch of salt. Slowly stir in milk, vanilla, and sugar until well-blended. Add cooked rice.
3. Pour into a 2-quart casserole dish and sprinkle grated nutmeg over the entire top. Place dish in a pan of water and bake at 375° for 55–60 minutes.

NOTE: *Another old-fashioned wonder from a wonderful generation!*

Index